Taking Charge

George Pierre Castile

Taking *C*harge

Native American Self-Determination and

Federal Indian Policy, 1975–1993

The University of Arizona Press   Tucson

The University of Arizona Press
© 2006 The Arizona Board of Regents
All rights reserved
This book is printed on acid-free, archival-quality paper.
Manufactured in the United States of America

11 10 09 08 07 06   6 5 4 3 2 1

Library of Congress Cataloging-in-Publication Data
Castile, George Pierre.
    Taking charge : Native American self-determination and federal
Indian policy, 1975–1993 / George Pierre Castile.
        p. cm.
    Includes bibliographical references and index.
    ISBN-13: 978-0-8165-2542-3 (hardcover : alk. paper)
    ISBN-10: 0-8165-2542-0 (hardcover : alk. paper)
        1. Indians of North America—Government relations. 2. Indians of
North America—Politics and government. 3. Self-determination,
National—United States. 4. Carter, Jimmy, 1924—Relations with
Indians. 5. Reagan, Ronald—Relations with Indians. 6. Bush,
George, 1924—Relations with Indians. I. Title.
E93.C349 2006
323.1197′07309048—dc22

                                    2006005785

To the Anthropology Department of the University of Arizona, who got me into all this. With thanks to its heads, faculty, students, and bozos.

Contents

Taking Charge

Introduction

Let me tell you just a little something about the American Indian in our land.

—Ronald Reagan

*I*n an earlier book, *To Show Heart: Native American Self-Determination and Federal Indian Policy, 1960–1975,* I attempted to examine the emergence of the Indian self-determination policy in the presidencies of Lyndon B. Johnson, Richard M. Nixon, and Gerald R. Ford, leading up to the Indian Self-Determination Act of 1975 (Castile 1998b). This book picks up where that one left off and seeks to explore what became of Indian policy in the following administrations of Jimmy Carter, Ronald Reagan, and George Bush.[1] The self-determination policy emerging in the sixties seemed to many to be a hopeful new departure in Indian affairs, restoring self-government to peoples whose community affairs had long been administered externally. How far those hopes have come toward being realized is one of the issues addressed here.

In this introduction I briefly reprise the history of the emergence of modern self-determination policy in the sixties and seventies, to provide a context for this book's coverage. The self-determination policy itself is only understandable in contrast to what went before, so for those who may be unfamiliar with the history of Indian affairs, I also provide a sketch of the major shifts in federal Indian policy, relevant to Indian self-governance, that led up to the modern state of affairs. The history of federal Indian policy from 1776 to 1975 is long but simple to summarize, since it is relatively uniform until 1934.[2]

From Self-Determination to Administered Communities

The native peoples of the Americas, like peoples everywhere, managed their own affairs for thousands of years, so why the necessity for a policy to restore self-government to their modern descendants? The question is of course rhetorical since, as we all know, starting in the 1600s, European states extended their hegemony over North America and incorporated the native peoples into their political systems. Even so, for some time, many of the peoples continued to manage their own affairs, since the Europeans did not so much incorporate them as encapsulate them. Very early on there was a tendency to isolate Indian peoples on lands "reserved" for their use, on which they adapted and continued their systems of self-governance as best they could.

From contact until the mid 1800s, the primary focus of Euro-American Indian policy was not on changing Indian ways but on how to persuade the Indians to accept the orderly transfer of Indian land to European hands and uses. The settlers saw Indians primarily as a hindrance to their agricultural harnessing of the "wilderness," an obstacle to be cleared away, much like wolves and trees. The founding fathers debated how to accomplish this process, whether by states or by federal government, by purchase and negotiation or by war and confiscation, but there was little debate about the necessity for the land to be transferred.

John Winthrop, first governor of Massachusetts colony, declared of Indian lands: "If we leave them sufficient for their use we may lawfully take the rest, there being more than enough for them and us" (quoted in Prucha 1962, 240). The law referred to was "natural law," as formulated by thinkers like John Locke, who declared the superior right to land ownership of civilized farmers over savage hunters (Williams 1990, 248). Although many Indian peoples along the eastern seaboard were partly agricultural, they were treated as if their mixed economies were entirely based on hunting and gathering, as if they were mere users of the commons, and thus not lawful owners of the land. John Wayne expressed a modern variant of this frontier doctrine: "I don't feel we did wrong in taking this great country away from them. There were great numbers of people who needed new land, and the Indians were selfishly trying to keep it for themselves" (Roberts and Olson 1995, 280).[3]

The independent United States continued and intensified quests for Indian lands. Many, including George Washington, himself a land speculator, thought that the question of Indians and their lands would solve itself. Indians would simply vanish, being incapable of surviving in contact with or of absorbing the benefits of Western civilization. In a letter to James Duane, Washington noted "the gradual extension of our settlements will as certainly cause the Savage as the Wolf to retire; both being beasts of prey though they differ in shape" (Prucha 2000, 1).[4] The Indian communities were in fact gradually swept ahead of the frontier as it expanded, until, in 1830, the Indian Removal Act was passed, which sought to move all remaining Indians to lands west of the Mississippi (Prucha 2000, 52). This wholesale removal policy was simply a logical extension of the more ad hoc land clearance that had preceded it.

Although there was considerable rhetoric among Europeans about civilizing and Christianizing the savages, little was actually done in Anglo-America. The policy of removal and reservation meant that the federal government took no real responsibility for internal affairs in Indian country. Thus, despite loss of land, population decline from introduced disease, and considerable economic and social disruption, surviving native communities continued to adapt their social structures as they saw fit, some, like the "civilized tribes" of the Southeast, with great success (Wallace 1993). But, as settlement continued to sweep into the trans-Mississippi West, the remaining Indians were, by the time of the Civil War, surrounded on their remaining reserved parcels of land—the reservations. Indian country was now unavoidably in the midst of the developing nation, and its inhabitants could no longer simply be left to their own devices.

In the name of civilization and assimilation, it was here, in the mid-nineteenth century, that individual Indian communities increasingly fell under direct federal administration, first by the military and then by the Indian service (Castile 1974). The Indian polities on the reservations, whatever their previous nature—band, tribe, chiefdom, or state—became governed by non-Indians in accord with non-Indian ideas of government. There emerged an era that Edward H. Spicer calls the "superintendency," which he characterizes as the "period of loss of self-determination" (Spicer 1969, 101). Not all reservation Indians had exactly the same experience, but all were placed under varying degrees of such supervision under federally appointed Indian agents.

Speaking of the Apache example, Spicer notes, "The reservation community became a small dictatorship. The superintendent maintained law and order. He with his staff of paid employees managed the tribally owned resources with some help from Indians whom he selected. There was no machinery of local government either to check the superintendent's decisions or to bring about participation in decision making by the Apaches" (Spicer 1969, 101–2). Spicer also notes, "Indians grew up in their communities under this system for a period of two generations or more, from the 1880s to the 1930s. Much of Indian life was increasingly colored by the undermining of Indian community organization and the substitution of government by administrative order. Two generations of Indians were schooled in the referral of decisions outside of family life to federal employees. They came to accept the situation as the nature of things."[5]

Not only were Indians not included in the federal governing process, native peoples' own governmental institutions were deliberately dismantled in a general program of deculturation and destructuring (Castile 1978). Theodore Roosevelt observed, "In my judgment the time has arrived when we should definitely make up our minds to recognize the Indian as an individual and not as a member of a tribe. The General Allotment Act is a mighty pulverizing engine to break up the tribal mass" (Castile 1979, 227). The General Allotment, or Dawes, Act of 1887, sought to give each Indian individual ownership of a piece of reservation land, much as the Homestead Act of the same era did for whites (Prucha 2000, 170). Any reservation land left over after allotments were made would be sold to needy settlers to defray the costs of educating and equipping the new Indian yeoman farmers, and the reservations as such would cease to exist.

This program of forced assimilation was at least an improvement on the racist notions of Indians' inherent savagery and incapacity to civilize that had preceded it. Indians were no longer doomed to vanish like wolves; they had only to give up being Indians. After the civil war, abolitionists had turned their attention to assimilating ex-slaves, who had previously been thought to be irrevocably slaves by nature. These same Christian reformers extended their efforts to the assimilation of the Indians, who had been thought to be irrevocably savages by nature (Prucha 1976). Frederick E. Hoxie has noted of the era, "The nation would make Native Americans the same offer it extended to other groups: membership in society in exchange for adapting to existing cultural standards" (1984, 34). These policies did not go as planned.

By the 1920s ex-slaves found themselves culturally but not structurally assimilated, held at the bottom of American society by the castelike system of segregation. Indians too had undergone considerable cultural reorientation, but most remained on the reservations, which were still federally administered. It became increasingly clear that the Dawes Act and the superintendency had as their primary effect the reduction of the reservation peoples to more or less complete economic and political dependency. Since all means of organization for self-help had been dismantled and their resource base fragmented, the Bureau of Indian Affairs (BIA) was now maintaining a client population that appeared to be permanently suspended at poverty level. The mighty pulverizing engine had failed, but there seemed to be no clear alternative, except to continue the policy of administration.

By the 1920s the Indian population had reached its low point; those that remained were largely isolated on remote western reservations. Indians might have been politically ignored except for public attention brought about by scandals in the Department of the Interior in 1922, when Secretary Albert Fall threatened Pueblo lands with the Bursum bill (Prucha 2000, 216). The Indian cause was then taken up by a mixture of the old Christian reformers and an artistic-intellectual elite who had discovered the romance of the pueblos at Taos. Of this Taos colony, a local noted, "Some painted pictures, some wrote books, and poems, and they all went nuts about something: ruins or Indian dances, old Mexican plays or tin sconces" (Kelly 1983, 116). One of these, a utopian socialist and former settlement-house worker, John Collier, had found in the Pueblos an idealized communalism, a "Red Atlantis," and it was he who organized the resistance to the assault on the Pueblo lands (Kelly 1983, 218).

The result of the Pueblo furor was a great deal of public attention to Indian affairs, which spawned a government-sponsored study, *The Problem of Indian Administration* (Merriam 1928). This found the reservation peoples, on all indices of social health, in bad shape. The blame was placed on failures of the Indian service, but in terms of failures to succeed in implementing assimilation policy, not failures in the policy itself. Like the earlier assimilationists, they declared, "The object of work with or for the Indians is to fit them either to merge into the social and economic life of the prevailing civilization as developed by the whites or to live in the presence of that civilization at least in accordance with a minimum standard of health and decency" (Merriam 1928, 86). Their recommendations aimed to improve the system of administration, not eliminate it.

There were glimmers of thinking that foreshadowed self-determination, for example, "Whichever way the individual Indians may elect to face, work in his behalf must be designed not to do for him but to help him do for himself" (Merriam 1928, 88), and "In every activity of the Indian Service the primary question should be, how is the Indian to be trained so that he will do this for himself. Unless this question can be clearly and definitely answered by the affirmative showing of distinct educational purpose and method the chances are the activity is impeding rather than helping the advancement of the Indian" (Merriam 1928, 89). But the "do for himself" theme was focused on the individual Indian, not the Indian community doing for its collective self.

A New Deal

Collier and other reformers continued to clamor for more fundamental change, generally seeking to move away from assimilation and toward the restoration, rather than the elimination, of Indian ways, all of which might well have gone nowhere except for the impact of the Great Depression and the political changes that it ushered in. Franklin Delano Roosevelt and his New Deal set out to address the social and economic woes of the nation as a whole, and a new deal for the Indians was included (Biolsi 1992; G. Taylor 1980). Collier became the instrument of this new deal as Indian commissioner in 1933 and set out to end "government absolutism" (Collier 1963, 130). Collier observed, "We tried to extend to the tribes a self-governing self-determination without any limit beyond the need to advance by stages to the goal" (1947, 263).

Called an "assault on assimilation" by one historian, the New Deal policy set out to reverse the course taken by the Dawes Act (Kelly 1983). The reformers' proposals for change were embodied in the Indian Reorganization Act of 1934 (IRA; Prucha 2000, 223; Deloria 2002). It was a wide-ranging bill, some of it concerned with stopping Indian land loss, other parts promising economic reform. As to self-determination, its opening title promised "to grant certain rights of home rule to Indians" (Prucha 2000, 223).[6] Section 16 of the bill provided the mechanism of reorganization to accomplish this home rule: "Any Indian tribe or tribes, residing on the same reservation, shall have the right to organize for its common welfare, and may adopt an appropriate constitution and by-laws" (Ibid., 224). Tribal councils with tribal chairs were the basic structure these constitutions created on most reservations.

In 1935 Collier optimistically predicted, "these constitutions and charters will give the Indians an assured and increasing part in the management of their own affairs and the direction of their lives. In the past such feeble organizations as were permitted to the Indians existed by administrative sufferance" (1935, 9). In fact, just as had the Christian reformers who opposed him, Collier set out to impose his own vision of proper community life on the Indians (Daily 2004). In his case, he aimed to restore on the reservations the "Red Atlantis," which he imagined he had discovered at Taos pueblo (Philp 1977, 2).[7] Collier, for example, encouraged economic communalism where it had never existed and was not wanted by the tribes. Governments were created, but the IRA constitutions were based on models drawn up by BIA lawyers, not locally cobbled together from scratch. All of the tribal governments were more alike than not, and the new governments were scarcely "Indian" if by that one means some form of traditional precontact organization (Castile 2004, 273).

The new IRA governments' authority was very limited: They did not have power over federal funds spent on the reservations, nor over the BIA staff, who continued to run things day to day. The overriding authority of the reservation superintendents remained and was upheld by Collier, who declared, "We must think of our superintendents as the representative of the entire Indian organization. Things coming here should come through the superintendent and Washington should not have independent dealing with the tribal councils" (G. Taylor 1980, 118). In fact, the amount of actual authority wielded by IRA councils was almost entirely dependent on the ideas of the particular reservation superintendent in charge (Wesley 1954).

Despite Collier's good intentions, in the end the new IRA tribal governments were still "feeble organizations" that "existed by administrative sufferance" (Collier 1935, 9). What he had created were the forms of self-government without the actual authority of government.[8] During Collier's era the councils governed very little and were generally little more than advisory bodies, allowed only to ratify decisions made, as before, by the bureau. They were instruments of the superintendency rather than substitutes for it, and the communities largely remained externally administered. Nonetheless, there were now Indian political structures where there had been none, and these had at least the potential to become instruments of tribal collective will, if circumstances should change to offer them real power.

From New Deal Back to Old Deal

Whatever its virtues or faults, this experiment in restructuring the Indian communities was short lived—only six years from the passage of the IRA in 1934 to 1940, when the political climate undermined support for Collier's reforms (G. Taylor 1980, 139). Entry into World War II in 1941 moved the BIA to the periphery of interest for the Roosevelt administration, even physically moving it out of Washington to Chicago to make room for wartime agencies (Philp 1999, 2). The Depression had created New Deal social engineering; the war turned attention away from social reform of all sorts, including Collier's, and he resigned by 1945. After the war, Indian policy shifted again, but this time to a theme commonly called "termination," which lasted from 1945 into the 1960s (Burt 1982; Fixico 1986; Philp 1999; Metcalf 2002).

Like New Deal Indian policies, termination had its political impetus outside of Indian affairs per se. It was in large part a reflection of a general postwar push toward reducing federal spending. The Hoover commission, exploring such cuts, recommended that spending on Indian affairs be reduced by entirely eliminating the Indian service and the trust relationship (Townsend 2000, 224). Termination policy also reflected the emerging civil rights movement. Many, including President Harry Truman, thought reservations were simply a form of segregation, to be eliminated like the others (Castile 1998b, xxii). Rather than by external reformers like Collier, this drive toward termination was pursued by Congress itself, especially two congressmen, Senator Arthur Watkins and Representative E. Y. Berry (Metcalf 2002; Schulte 1984).

The result, by 1953, was a general repudiation of Collier's approach and a congressional declaration of its new-old direction. This was embodied in House Concurrent Resolution 108, which declared the aim of Congress to make Indians "subject to the same laws and privileges and responsibilities as are applicable to other citizens of the United States, to end their status as wards of the United States," and to free them "from Federal supervision and control" (Prucha 2000, 234). It was essentially the same as the assimilation-era offer of "membership in society in exchange for adapting to existing cultural standards" (Hoxie 1984, 34). Like Collier, the terminationists spoke of Indian self-determination, but they meant something very different by it (Philp 1999, 94). Termination would result in a sort of self-determination, but self-determination only in concert with their non-Indian neighbors.

Once Indian communities had their special federal relation terminated, their governance would become entirely their own affair, but within the legal context of the states in which they were located. Former reservations would become incorporated into municipalities and counties within the states, where Indians would share governance with their non-Indian neighbors.[9] Some would move far away from the former reservations, under a program called "relocation," in which Indians were to be actively recruited and assisted to leave their rural homes and find employment in urban areas. Donald Lee Fixico notes, "Relocating Native Americans would help to achieve the goal of termination by removing them from the source of their cultural existence" (1986, 183). Other rural populations after the war were moving into the cities; Indians would join them, and those that remained behind would merge with non-Indians.

Thus, as under the Dawes-era assimilation scheme, termination was expected to lead to the complete elimination of distinct Indian communities under federal administration. In opposition to it, Indians became increasingly active in attempting to influence national-level Indian policy. Political activity by individual leaders had always existed, but the IRA government structures gave it a mechanism for collective expression. In both the United States and Canada, World War II took many Indians off the reservations to fight or to work in labor-short war industries, and the returning veterans brought a new, wider perspective to Indian politics (Bernstein 1991; Townsend 2000; R. Sheffield 2004). This generally increased level of Indian political activism led among other things to the formation in 1945 of the National Congress of American Indians (NCAI), the first pan-Indian national lobbyist organization (Bernstein 1991, 112; Cowger 1999).[10]

Ironically, the terminationist attempts to eliminate Indian communities appear to have fueled a political revitalization that strengthened them. Nagel notes, "These conflicts, while often immobilizing and long lived, nevertheless galvanized many lethargic reservation communities, as groups and factions organized themselves for political action in tribal governments" (Nagel 1997, 119). Despite congressional pressure, remarkably few reservations actually had their federal status ended, as Prucha notes: "The Indians in the terminated groups numbered 13,263 out of an estimated tribal Indian population of 400,000 or not much more than 3 percent of federally recognized Indians" (1984, 1058). This was in considerable part due to tribal resistance, but the termination policy also simply began to run out of political support by the early sixties (Prucha 1984, 1056).

From Termination to the 1975 Self-Determination Act

Termination had flourished in an era of cost cutting and reduction of the New Deal social programs. In the sixties that background was gone, replaced by a new wave of social experimentation and spending that in the administration of LBJ rivaled and even surpassed that of the New Deal (Heclo 1986; Matusow 1984, ch. 4). By 1964 the civil rights movement was triumphant, and assimilation leading to the elimination of ethnic groups was no longer the dominant theme in minority relations, mosaic having replaced melting pot as metaphor (Weisbrot 1990).[11] The civil rights movement, which had been interpreted to support termination, now seemed to argue against it, all of which militated against termination as a policy but didn't offer any practical direction as an alternative, except the status quo, which was also unsatisfactory (Castile 1998b, 176).

The political visibility of the Indians also changed: The sixties counterculture had discovered and exalted the Indian, or at least their own romantic version of Indian life (Brand 1988). In addition to the civil rights movement, social activism of all sorts was on the rise, in what some collectively called "the movement" (Anderson 1995). Riding these waves of public attention and using the demonstration tactics of the civil rights movement, mostly urban Indian activists drew still more attention to things Indian, starting with a sit-in at Alcatraz Island in 1969 (Johnson 1996; Nagel 1997). But even as this wave of activism arose, a new direction in Indian policy had already quietly emerged.

In 1964 President Lyndon Baines Johnson declared war on poverty and set out to create the Great Society (Castile 1998b, ch. 2). Johnson was even more ambitious than his mentor FDR, as a biographer noted: "Johnson talked about a perfect America. He seemed to want to solve all of its problems susceptible to political correction and do it now" (Conkin 1986, 209). The instrument he created to carry out his war was the Office of Economic Opportunity (OEO), and within it the Community Action Program (CAP; Patterson 1994). What was new about the CAP approach was that it set out not to "do for" the poor but to organize the communities of the poor to do for themselves, through federal grants made directly to them. Community action agencies were to be formed in poverty communities with "maximum feasible participation" from among the poor; as one observer notes, "community action would seek to reform institutions by empowering the poor" (Matusow 1984, 245).

The original focus of CAP was the urban ghetto, but this focus was expanded to include the rural poor, and thus the reservations (Cobb 1998). Since the CAP approach circumvented local and state governments to deal directly with the organized poor, it soon ran into considerable political resistance from those bypassed levels of government. On the reservations, however, a direct federal to local government relationship already existed; the only political constituency the OEO circumvented was another federal agency, the BIA. In general society, the radical approach of empowerment was soon reined in, and the OEO was reduced to a more traditional provider of services through established channels.[12] But on the reservations the impact of this brief experiment was much greater and longer lasting.

As we have seen, tribal governments had existed since the Collier era but had no direct control over reservation funds and resources. Federal funds on reservations had always been distributed through the filter of the BIA, but now the OEO made grants directly to Indian community action agencies, who controlled and administered them, including hiring and firing. Here was a remarkable new experience for the reservation leaders and one that came to stimulate a new direction in Indian self-government.

Not only did tribes embrace the OEO programs, but they began to draw contrasts between the approach of the bureau and that of the poverty warriors. The director of the NCAI, Vine Deloria Jr., noted in 1967, "The Poverty program is extremely popular and for the first time tribes can plan and run their own programs for their people without someone in the BIA dictating to them" (Castile 1998b, 41). D'Arcy McNickle, a founder of the NCAI, noted of the OEO that its "transferal of authority and responsibility for decision making to the local community was an administrative feat which the Bureau of Indian Affairs, after more than one hundred years of stewardship, had never managed to carry out" (1973, 119).

The bureau had a rocky relationship with the OEO, but some of its more thoughtful members also began to draw lessons from the experience. William King, superintendent at Salt River, wrote to Secretary of the Interior Stewart Udall in 1966, "We, in BIA, if we are wise, will learn a great deal from these positive aspects of the OEO program on the reservations" (Castile 1998b, 48). King in the same memo proposed the OEO grant and contract procedures as a model to be emulated, calling "for the government to contract with the tribes to carry out many of the activities presently performed by the Bureau" (Ibid.). Udall circulated these ideas in the bureau and elsewhere, and the phrase self-determination began to be applied to them.

The rhetoric, the language of self-determination, had long been around; what was new was a practical mechanism to transfer authority to the tribes—the OEO system of compacting with local Indian community action agencies to carry out federal programs. This had demonstrated how the thing might be done, and Udall and his staff began translating it into their administration of Indian affairs (Castile 1998b, ch. 3). Some in Congress continued to support the termination doctrine, especially Senator Henry Jackson of Washington State, but Udall pressed the new idea directly to President Johnson. Johnson was eventually persuaded and endorsed the approach in his "Forgotten American" message to Congress in 1968: "I propose a new goal for our Indian programs: A goal that ends the old debate about 'termination' and stresses self-determination."[13]

Johnson had apparently embraced the new policy because he regarded it as a success story for his Great Society program, as he noted in his address. For some time Udall and the bureau attempted to carry out tribal contracting using their existing authority, but what was needed was new legislation (Castile 1998b, 56). Although Udall and others drew up such legislative proposals, Johnson's Indian message unfortunately had come near the end of his administration and was never translated into law (Ibid., 71). By 1968 Indian self-determination had been declared a desirable policy and mechanisms for implementation were at hand, but a new administration, that of Richard M. Nixon, would have to take it to the next stage.

This seemed unlikely since the Nixon administration was generally hostile to the Johnson Great Society programs and set out to dismantle many of them, including the OEO. But despite this overall change in domestic policy direction, the Indian self-determination policy won approval and endorsement early on. Whether for personal or political reasons, Richard M. Nixon is probably the only president in modern times to take a strong interest in Indian affairs (Castile 1998b, 74). His aide Robert Haldeman noted, "He feels very strongly that we need to show more heart, and that we care about people, and thinks the Indian problem is a good area for us to work in" (Castile 1998b, 76).

In 1970 Nixon sent a special Indian message to Congress, which like LBJ's endorsed "self-determination without termination." His version also proposed specific legislation "which would empower a tribe or a group of tribes or any other Indian community to take over the control or operation of Federally funded or administered programs . . . whenever the tribal council or comparable community governing group decided to do so."[14] While he acknowledged the success of OEO programs on the reservations, the devolution of power to local communities was also consistent with his own larger domestic policy theme of New Federalism, stressing decentralization of government, "in which power, funds and responsibility will flow from Washington to the states and to the people."[15] In this case, the Indian people.

Unfortunately, Nixon was engaged in what some have called a "war" with a Congress controlled by the Democratic Party (Ambrose 1991, 59). As a result, "Most of the administration's Indian reform initiatives . . . got bogged down in the congressional stalemate machine" (Garment 1997,

227). Although hearings were held in 1972, his self-determination legislation was not passed in the Nixon years, and the administration had
to operate throughout using existing legislation (Castile 1998b, 106, 156).
However, the basic idea of Indian self-determination was not unpalatable
to the Democratic Congress, and once Nixon was out of the picture, it
passed easily.

Senator Henry Jackson had by 1972 shifted to support of self-determination, and it was he who sponsored the legislation that became the
Indian Self-Determination and Educational Assistance Act, signed into
law by President Gerald R. Ford in 1975 (Prucha 2000, 275; Castile 1998b,
169). Only slightly different than Nixon's proposals, it was "An act to provide maximum Indian participation in the Government and education
of Indian people" that declared "the establishment of a meaningful Indian self-determination policy which will permit an orderly transition
from federal domination of programs for and services to Indians to effective and meaningful participation by the Indian people in the planning,
conduct, and administration of those programs and services" (Prucha
2000, 275). It then spelled out how grants and contracts would be made
in furtherance of these aims.

Gerald Ford's administration had little time to act on the legislation, since he was shortly thereafter narrowly defeated for reelection. This
book thus begins the story of the implementation of self-determination
in the presidency of Jimmy Carter, first to inherit the new approach.

Keeping Faith

The Carter Administration

*B*efore assuming the presidency, James Earl Carter had little experience with Indian affairs. It was not a concern when he was governor of Georgia, his home state having eliminated the Indian policy issue by eliminating the bulk of the Georgia Indian population in the 1830s removal period (Wallace 1993). Indeed some of Carter's own family holdings appear to have been based on lands distributed by lottery after the forcible removal of the Creek from those lands (Bourne 1997, 9). His biographer notes of Carter's childhood on the former Creek lands, "They regularly searched for Indian arrowheads; ghosts of the evicted Creeks were very much in Jimmy's mind as he grew up" (Bourne 1997, 26). But they were not apparently very much on his mind by the time he became president. His autobiographical account of his presidency, *Keeping Faith*, does not even mention the topic (Carter 1982).

During the 1976 presidential campaign, the Carter staff made some attempt to reach out to Indian leaders, especially the National Congress of American Indians (NCAI) and the National Tribal Chairmen's Association (NTCA).[1] Carter met briefly with some of these leaders, and his representative David Berg held a debate with Bradley Patterson, a Nixon-Ford White House Indian policy expert, at the NCAI convention on October 20, 1976.[2] His staff drew up a draft position paper on Indian affairs, which endorsed the policy and theme of self-determination already in force. "It is time that the Federal government recognized that the Indian tribes have the right to determine the course of their lives, and that the majority of decisions affecting tribal lives should be made in tribal council rooms not Washington DC."[3]

But this statement also echoed his theme of reorganizing government and cutting its costs, one of his top priorities as president. "Draw-

ing from the experience of his most celebrated prepresidential achieve-
ment—the reorganization of the Georgia state government—Carter set
out to impose order and efficiency on the federal government" (Sugrue
1998, 141). Indians were to be included in this streamlining. "As part of my
plan to reorganize the Federal government I intend to thoroughly review
the delivery of programs to Indians . . . to eliminate waste, inefficiency
and duplication."[4] This was potentially in contradiction to the endorsement of self-determination, and was reminiscent of the termination era.

National-level attempts to cut government spending have histori-
cally tended to have a disproportionate impact on Indian communities,
which are far more dependent on federal funding than others are. How
Indian self-determination was to be pursued efficiently and on the cheap
was not made clear; what was clear was that Indian policy was once again
being fitted into a larger presidential domestic policy theme (Castile 1992,
171). Where Johnson had embraced Indian self-determination in the context of his War on Poverty, Nixon had seen it as a form of New Federalism, and now Carter proposed to make it an exemplar of his reengineer-
ing of government.

Early in the Carter presidency, it did appear as if there would be some
significant activity regarding Indian matters. In his 1970 Presidential Indian Message, Nixon had called for legislative creation of an assistant
secretary of the interior for Indian affairs, but like many of his proposals,
this was stalled in a Democratic Congress (Castile 1998b, 95). Carter did
create the job, however, six months into his administration, in July of
1977, by executive order. Forest J. Gerard, former aide to Senator Henry
Jackson, was the first to hold the office (Prucha 1984, 1123). The idea for
this action, James Officer suggests, originated with Carter's secretary of
the interior, Cecil Andrus: "Andrus had discovered that he could abolish
one of the existing assistant secretary positions and replace it with the
Indian job" (Officer 1984, 94).

McCool suggests this was done in the context of efforts to resolve
Indian water rights: "In order to appease Indian interests, the secretary
of Interior appointed the first assistant secretary for Indian affairs" (1994,
229). However, since it was done almost immediately in the new administration, it could hardly have been responsive to actions not yet taken in
water rights resolution. More likely the repositioning of the BIA, already

on the table, simply offered itself as something easy to accomplish in the administration's high-priority area of government reorganization. As with Nixon's pursuit of New Federalism, what could not be easily accomplished on a national scale could be "demonstrated" through the reservation system, which was susceptible to simple federal fiat.

Once this first step was taken, further change bogged down. Andrus created an Interior task force to look into further reorganization of the BIA, but its recommendations appear not to have been implemented (Prucha 1984, 1123). Having created the new post of assistant secretary and as part of the streamlining effort, the administration planned to eliminate the venerable office of commissioner of Indian affairs, in existence since 1824 (Kvasnicka and Viola 1979). It was the new assistant secretary, Forest Gerard, who insisted that the post be retained, commenting in his eventual letter of resignation, "I am also gratified that you and Secretary Andrus recognized the importance of maintaining the post of Commissioner of Indian Affairs to oversee the day to day operation work of the Bureau of Indian Affairs."[5] William E. Hallett, a Red Lake Chippewa, took office as commissioner in December 1979, just as Gerard, who had championed the position, was resigning (Prucha 1984, 1124). The post of commissioner was not filled in the Reagan administration or subsequent administrations, making Hallett the last in that long line.[6]

Other changes were considered: The NTCA proposed "the appointment of an Indian as a Special Assistant to the President on Indian affairs." Presidential staff commented, "If the President appoints a Special Assistant for one area or interest group, he will be pressured to do so for others."[7] This position was never created. Other attempts were made at fresh approaches to Indian matters, including an "intergovernmental relations network," but no significant structural changes were accomplished.[8] Emma Gross notes, "Access may . . . . be provided Indian interests through special councils and commissions whose purpose it is to provide a forum for Indian views and develop proposals for change. Presidential administrations since Kennedy, except for Carter, have established such councils and commissions" (1989, 64).

In line with his cost cutting and consolidation themes, Carter's administration also proposed to transfer Indian education from Interior to the newly created Department of Education, but many Indians opposed the move (Prucha 1984, 1142).[9] A staff member wrote to the president, "Letters and telegrams to you and the senior staff have expressed the concern that transfer of these programs would lead to the erosion of BIA, which for all their dissatisfaction with it—they view as 'their' agency."[10] This was not an irrational fear, since the last time major functions were transferred from the bureau to other agencies, primarily health, was in the context of the fifties drive for termination (Burt 1982, 55). The Carter staff prepared a response, saying in his name, "Let me assure you that this transfer is not intended to change in any way any of these special relationships existing under treaty law."[11] The proposed move died for lack of support in Congress.

Within the White House, Indian matters seem to have fallen primarily to Stuart E. Eizenstat, assistant to the president for domestic affairs and policy. Midge Costanza, head of the White House Office for Public Liaison, was also a participant. But White House involvement was minimal since Carter had a tendency to abdicate his policy responsibility to his cabinet officers (Warshaw 1997). Eizenstat, in a letter to Representative Donald Fraser, wrote, "Consistent with the President's policy of Cabinet government, the primary responsibility for Indian affairs therefore resides in the Interior Department, where Secretary Andrus and his appointees have placed a very high priority on protection of Indian rights, and to the extent feasible, the righting of past wrongs. When questions do arise at the White House concerning Indian affairs, Kathy Fletcher of my staff and Marilyn Haft of Midge Costanza's staff are the proper contact people" (Eizenstat 1997).[12] This shift toward decentralizing power from the White House, where it had been concentrated by Nixon, began under Ford.

The arrangement was not popular in Indian country. LaDonna Harris complained, "every time we approached the White House about an Indian issue we were told 'That's Andrus' responsibility.'"[13] There is no indication, however, that the secretary of the interior, Cecil Andrus, in fact took any particular personal interest in Indian affairs, although he did call for an administration review of its Indian policy.[14] He, like Carter, does not even mention Indian affairs in his memoirs (Andrus and Connelly 1998). Indians from past experience were disinclined to accept the notion that Interior and the BIA might be the best place to take their issues.

The effect of this buck passing from White House to cabinet was a kind of acephalous domestic program, including Indian policy. The administration was not particularly active in pursuing programs for any minorities or their civil rights, despite some promising early rhetoric (Califano 1981, 228; Graham 1998, 202). Hugh Davis Graham comments on Carter's civil rights policy: "Policy entrepreneurs in Congress and the subpresidency shaped the development of civil rights policy during the Carter administration much more than had the president" (1998, 216). This was true of Indian policy as well. One such policy entrepreneur in Indian affairs was Morris (Mo) Udall, of Arizona (who had fought Carter for the presidential nomination). He, for example, more or less single-handedly pushed through federal recognition for the Tucson Pascua Yaqui in 1978 (Castile 2002).

The Presidential Indian Message

LBJ had been the first president since Grant to issue a presidential Indian message, in 1968, a precedent followed by Nixon in 1970. But neither Ford nor Carter issued such messages (Castile 1998b). Forest Gerard did early on propose the writing of such a message, saying, "As a new administration, we have the opportunity to disassociate ourselves from some of the devastating and unpopular policies and practices of the Nixon-Ford administrations and to formulate more constructive policy in light of contemporary Indian issues."[15] This is a curious statement since the Nixon-Ford policy was, as we have seen, self-determination, and it was widely popular in Indian country (Castile 1998b). Cecil Andrus wrote to the president suggesting that Interior draw up an Indian policy statement: "It could then be circulated to other Cabinet departments for review and comment before being finalized and resubmitted for your consideration."[16]

Eizenstat at first proposed a wider ranging approach: "We treat this subject under the Domestic Policy Review system, so that all concerned agencies have input at the beginning."[17] The Office of Management and Budget (OMB) indicated that it had already looked into the Indian policy question and was pessimistic, saying, "We question whether it is desirable, given the complexity of the problems and the unlikelihood of reaching solutions satisfactory to Indians and non-Indians alike, to have a high White House profile on Indian policy studies this year."[18] Eizenstat agreed and deferred the review and writing of a policy statement to Interior: "This is an internal job in Interior."[19]

The lack of a presidential policy statement caused a group of Indian leaders to complain, "Your administration has been in office more than 14 months without announcing an Indian policy."[20] LaDonna Harris, noting Indian unhappiness with the Carter administration, suggested, "One way to help the situation is for the President to make a major policy statement, as Presidents Johnson and Nixon did in the past."[21] Bee notes, "By avoiding a comprehensive declaration of Indian policy, the Carter staff left observers with one of two conclusions . . . either the president had not made up his mind or the president did not want to get caught by the backlash in a congressional election year when several important Democrats in western states were fighting for their political lives" (1982, 95).

In his 1978 State of the Union address Carter made a one-paragraph utterance on Native Americans, which was as close as he ever came to a presidential Indian message. "This administration has acted consistently to uphold its trusteeship responsibility to Native Americans. We have also elevated the post of commissioner of Indian Affairs to the level of assistant secretary of Interior. In 1978, the administration will review federal Native American policy and will step up efforts to help tribes assess and manage their natural resources."[22]

In the 1979 State of the Union, he made a similar brief statement:

The federal government has a special responsibility to Native Americans, and I intend to continue to exercise this responsibility fairly and sensitively. My administration will continue to seek negotiated settlements to difficult conflicts over land, water, and other resources and will ensure that the trust relationship and self-determination principles continue to guide Indian policy. There are difficult conflicts which occasionally divide Indian and non-Indian citizens in this country. We will seek to exercise leadership to resolve these problems equitably and compassionately.[23]

Despite Indian concerns, by the end of 1978 the Carter White House had already decided not to make any formal presidential Indian policy statement at all. Citing various problems, Eizenstat said, "These concerns led Interior to withdraw its request some months ago for the administration to do an Indian policy review and to prepare a policy statement. Briefly, the issues are so politically tough that if we were to come out anywhere in the middle we would find ourselves without a constituency and without having made much progress in solving Indian related problems."[24] Absent a presidential message, the policy of self-determination remained in place by default, but never seems to have gotten a clear endorsement by the Carter domestic policy staff. Indian matters were dealt with piecemeal, most staff time focusing on the issue of Indian claims. The White House staff was aware of its lack of success with Indian policy. A staff memo on the Tribally Controlled Community College Assistance Act notes, "The above bill is virtually the only thing we are doing that Indians have requested."[25]

Indian Claims

Early on in the administration arose the issue of Indian claims to land, fishing rights, and the like, which had increasingly been pressed in the courts.[26] In this as in other areas, the Carter administration seems to have sought compromise through negotiations. An aide wrote to the attorney general, "At the request of the president, I met with Senator Henry Jackson . . . to discuss his general ideas concerning future handling of these claims. . . . Senator Jackson suggests that a task force be organized to try to establish some mechanism for handling all of these matters, outside of the courts, and under some uniform set of guidelines."[27] Such a task force was established, but no consistent guidelines or policy seem to have developed (Fay Cohen 1986, 102).

Judging by the presidential library files, probably the greatest amount of staff time was devoted to the single issue of the settlement of eastern Indian land claims. This issue had arisen through court decisions in the Ford administration, notably *Passamaquoddy Tribe v. Morton,* which upheld the federal government's obligation to pursue Indian claims against the state of Maine for lands unlawfully taken in defiance of the 1790 Trade and Intercourse Act (Prucha 1984, 1173; 2000, 277). When this obligation was upheld on appeal in 1976, the Ford administration sidestepped the issue, leaving it to Carter. Ford aide Bradley Patterson said, "Mr. Carter, then as President, will have to make the final judgment about what kind of lawsuits or a legislative package to support" (Castile 1998b, 173).

The claims were potentially highly disruptive, clouding title to as much as half of Maine lands. Carter approached this problem as he did most, as a matter for negotiation rather than litigation. He appointed an inter-agency working group to meet with the Maine tribes, and on February 10, 1978, they announced an agreement to introduce legislation in Congress to settle the claims, paying some $25 million, granting certain tracts of land, and extending federal recognition and services to the tribes.[28] After further discussion, a substantially similar version was approved by the tribes and the state of Maine and finally took the form of the Maine Indian Claims Settlement Act on October 10, 1980 (Prucha 2000, 297).[29]

This set no clear policy direction, however; some other claims, such as that of the Indians of Rhode Island, were similarly settled, but that of the Mashpee went to the courts, where the Mashpee lost (Prucha 1984, 1175; Campisi 1991). The land dispute between the Hopi and Navajo, which had begun long before the Carter administration, failed at ne-gotiation and dragged on beyond the administration (Kammer 1980).[30] Similarly, the long-standing Sioux claims over the loss of the Black Hills was decided by the Supreme Court in 1980, in *United States v. Sioux Nation of Indians*, but the dispute went on (Lazarus 1991).

Water Rights

Indian water rights derive from the 1908 case of *Winters v. United States*, in which the government was found to have created an "implied reser-vation" of water rights when it created Indian reservations (Pevar 2002, 240). Stephen L. Pevar notes, "The tribe is presumed to have a right to enough water to satisfy the reservation's purpose, that is, enough water to meet the tribe's present and future needs," but the process of determining just how much water is complex (2002, 240). Absent some clear quanti-fication, the reserved right remained largely theoretical for many years after 1908, few tribes receiving actual "wet water"; those who tried found themselves involved in costly litigation with their non-Indian neighbors.

As is often the case, what happened with Indian water was a reflection of policies aimed at non-Indian problems, as two students of Indian water policy agree. Daniel McCool notes, "Thus Indian water rights policy under the Carter administration was inextricably tied to the administration's efforts to modify the entirety of the federal government's water resource development policy" (1994, 228), and Thomas R. McGuire says, "The negotiation policy itself evolved in haphazard fashion during the Carter administration, a product of, more than an integral element in, the Western water policy reform movement" (1992, 230).

Indians were included in the general water policy message Carter sent to Congress, saying his policy would include "an instruction to Federal Agencies to work promptly and expeditiously to inventory and quantify Federal reserved and Indian water rights. In several areas of the country, States have been unable to allocate water because these rights have not been determined. This quantification effort should focus on high priority areas, should include close consultation with the States and water users and should emphasize negotiations rather than litigation wherever possible."[31] The problem being addressed is not so much the delivery of water to the reservations as it is the cloud those undefined rights throw on non-Indian water rights, much as Indian claims did on Maine land titles.

Carter's attempts to reform western water policy encountered considerable opposition, not only from Indians, especially the NCAI, but more importantly from western state congressional delegations (McCool 1994, 231). Negotiations between states and Indians in most cases were not successful: "The two exceptions were the Ak-Chin bill and the Fallon bill. But both of these reservations are very small (21,840 acres and 8,120 acres, respectively) and the amount of water involved was not large" (Ibid., 233). In the end, as with many of Carter's policies, little was accomplished to reform federal water policy. "With few exceptions President Carter failed to resolve the controversy over western water rights" (Ibid., 232).

Fishing Rights

Carter's policy of negotiation also failed to settle the question of reserved Indian fishing rights, which had been established by the Boldt decision of 1974 (*United States v. Washington*), but which were much disputed by

Washington State (Castile 1982, 1985). Carter established a task force in 1977 to examine the controversy and make some sort of compromise recommendations (Fay Cohen 1986, 101; Prucha 1984, 1185). However, as Fay Cohen notes of the recommendations made in 1978, "Nobody liked the plan. The tribes, the fisherman's associations, and the state all rejected it" (1986, 104). With the failure of the negotiation doctrine, the dispute moved to the courts. The administration was considerably divided over whether to support Supreme Court review of *United States v. Washington*, but in the end, it was supported (Fay Cohen 1986, 108). The outcome in 1979 was *Washington v. Washington State Commercial Passenger Fishing Vessel Association,* in which the Boldt decision was finally upheld by the Supreme Court (Getches, Wilkinson, and Williams 1998, 882).

Despite Carter's attempts to avoid the courts, it was a time of significant judicial activity in Indian affairs. In 1978 the Supreme Court decided *Oliphant v. Suquamish Tribe, United States v. Wheeler,* and *Santa Clara Pueblo v. Martinez,* the first of which limited the extent of Indian sovereignty while the other two strengthened it (Prucha 2000, 285–87). In *Oliphant,* a non-Indian, Mark Oliphant, arrested on the Port Madison Reservation, claimed that he was not subject to tribal jurisdiction. The court agreed: "An examination of our earlier precedents satisfies us that, even ignoring treaty provisions and congressional policy, Indians do not have criminal jurisdiction over non-Indians absent affirmative delegation of such power by Congress" (Getches, Wilkinson, and Williams 1998, 536).

In *Wheeler* and in *Martinez* the court affirmed tribal sovereignty. A Navajo prosecuted in trial court and subsequently in federal court claimed double jeopardy. The court disagreed: "Since tribal and federal prosecutions are brought by separate sovereigns, they are not 'for the same offense,' and the Double Jeopardy Clause thus does not bar one when the other has occurred" (Getches, Wilkinson, and Williams 1998, 383). In *Martinez* a tribal member sued the tribe for violating the Indian Civil Rights Act. The court held that the suit was barred since "Indian tribes have long been recognized as possessing the common law immunity from suit traditionally enjoyed by sovereign powers" (Ibid., 511).

Austerity

Carter's larger scale domestic policy was surprisingly un-Democratic, that is to say, not typical of historical Democratic Party tendencies. One observer noted, "Although Carter had campaigned in the general elections as a liberal, he governed as a conservative" (Gillon 1992, 189). There seems a general consensus that Carter was neither a New Deal nor a Johnson liberal, with their characteristic bent toward extensive spending on social programs, but tended instead toward Republican-like austerity in the quest for a balanced budget (Leuchtenburg 1998, 16–17). Indian affairs were not exempt, so although the administration was theoretically committed to Indian self-determination, that commitment was threatened by underfunding. As we have seen, an inherent dilemma in Indian self-government is its dependency on federal funding, which the tribes cannot control or even predict reliably.

Senator James Abourezk complained in 1978 of a shortfall of funds to support Indian contracting under the self-determination policy, and a refusal by OMB to request additional funds. "If Indian self-determination is really at the heart of your administration's Indian policy, these contracts should receive your full support. To allow the OMB decision to remain as it is not only treats Indian contractors inequitably but deals self-determination a mortal blow."[32] The director of OMB responded, "I sincerely believe that you and I are in agreement on the importance to Indians of the Federal contracting program. . . . The Administration, however is also seriously committed to sound financial management at all levels of government. The President is particularly concerned, as you know, with maintaining the integrity of the Budget and with holding down Federal spending to the lowest possible levels."[33] This injunction to the tribes to make bricks without straw, or contracts without funds, veered in the direction of "termination by accountants," an accusation later leveled at the Reagan administration (C. Morris 1988). Eventually Congress did in fact "add on" some funds for the purpose of supporting self-determination contracts, despite administration opposition (Bee 1982, 187, 199).

Attempts at cutting costs of Indian social spending had begun with the Ford administration, continued with Carter, and in the Reagan years,

cuts in spending were even more vigorously pursued. This was not simply a reflection of more general cuts in social spending: "Overall Indian
spending has tended to go down over the full course of the FY 1975–1999
period, while overall federal non-defense spending has gone up" (CRS
1998, 180; Stuart 1990, 8). One result of all this for Indians is "rights without resources" (Stull, Schultz, and Cadue 1986). As discussed in the next
chapter, Congress was passing a good deal of legislation favorable to Indian interests but largely of a symbolic nature. While Indians gained a say
over archaeological finds and access to sacred sites, federal money spent
on their basic needs declined.

Another of Carter's austerity themes was energy conservation, but
the Native American Council of Energy Resource Tribes (CERT), an
OPEC-like group formed in 1975, received little attention. Navajo Peter
MacDonald, CERT chair, noted, "During this period President Jimmy
Carter called a Camp David summit on the energy crisis. . . . The Indians however were excluded. . . . We had formed a coalition, yet no one
paid any attention to us" (1993, 228). LaDonna Harris complained that
when CERT representatives went to the White House staff to discuss their
problems, "they were immediately told they would have to work through
the BIA. The tribes were there, of course, to explain that the BIA had been
the source of most of those problems."[34]

There was another "resource" development that went virtually un-
noticed by the Carter administration. As the tribes began to develop
more effective and assertive government in the sixties and seventies,
some tribal leaders were testing the limits of their sovereignty in relation
to the states, in a search for new sources of tribal revenue. Pevar notes,
"The U.S. Constitution gives Congress exclusive authority over certain
subjects, and Indian affairs is one of them. Therefore, as a general rule,
a state may not enforce its laws on reservation Indians without express
congressional consent" (2002, 119).

This freedom from state regulation and taxation might potentially
be a source of tribal revenue, and one of several leaders exploring this potential was Harold Tommie, Seminole tribal council chair in 1975 (Kersey
1996, 120). The Seminole became involved in court battles with the state
of Florida, initially over sales of cigarettes, free of state tax, but ultimately
and more importantly, by 1979, over the legality of tribally run bingo

games (Kersey 1996, 127). This was not to be resolved until well into the Reagan administration, when Indian gaming began to emerge as a highly significant resource.

The Carter administration had so little success in implementing any of its policy initiatives that most evaluations of the Carter presidency have tended to judge it as an overall failure, though some of the more recent evaluations have been kinder (Dumbrell 1993; Fink and Graham 1998; Jones 1988; Kaufman 1993; Rosenbaum and Ugrinsky 1997). One of his harshest critics was Joseph A. Califano Jr., his own secretary of Health, Education, and Welfare (HEW), who complained not only of Carter's inept leadership in social policy, but also of his lack of candor: "My God, there is some Elmer Gantry in this born again President, I thought" (1981, 407).

Absent a clear White House agenda in Indian affairs, Indian policy continued without focus, in what Bee has called "policy ad hoccery" (Bee 1992, 140). Vine Deloria noted, "Neither Carter nor Reagan disturbed the status of tribal governments with new policy considerations" (1984, 7). Alvin M. Josephy suggests "the Carter administration, in a somewhat confusing manner, dealt with Indians as if they were no different from the rest of the population and flirted for a while with the notion of ending the government's historic trust obligation to the tribes" (1988, 271). I have found nothing in the Carter papers to support this last assertion of an intent to abrogate the trust relation. Senator Abourezk, not the administration, did toy with the idea of eliminating the BIA and simply distributing its funds per capita directly to the tribes. He remarks, "I am not so sure the suggestion of direct payments to the Indians shouldn't be considered more seriously" (Abourezk 1989, 204).

In general Indian leaders did not feel well served by the Carter administration. LaDonna Harris notes, "the Nixon administration was more accessible. This is very disconcerting for a dyed in the wool Democrat."[35] Philip S. Deloria says, "The Carter administration, in my experience, was constantly in a state of embarrassment. Whatever it did with respect to Indians simply added more embarrassment to an already humiliating four years" (Philp 1986, 320). Joe De La Cruz comments on attempts to arrange a meeting with Indian leaders: "Carter never showed up for this meeting and the people he sent in to represent him did not want to listen to us" (Philp 1986, 312). Edward C. Johnson notes, "Unfortunately, the Carter administration never developed a comprehensive Indian policy. President Carter just allowed things to go on as usual. He did not take a great interest in Indian matters, and neither did his high level staff" (Philp 1986, 299).[36]

The year 1975 was not the only one that marked the formalization of self-determination as federal Indian policy, but it marked the beginning of a brief era of congressional legislative activism in Indian affairs that lasted until 1978. Congress, after the fall of Nixon, had enhanced its own grasp on the policy-making process at the expense of the presidency. Carter, a Democratic president, with a Democrat-dominated Congress, nonetheless found himself struggling to promote his legislative priorities—against Congress's own priorities. This was as true in Indian affairs as elsewhere (Jones 1988; Lammers and Genovese 2000, 255).

Significant events in Indian affairs were happening during the years of the Carter presidency: The American Indian Policy Review Commission (AIPRC) delivered its sweeping set of recommendations (1977), and the next year, 1978, was a landmark year, seeing the passage of the American Indian Religious Freedom Act, the establishment of the Federal Acknowledgment Process, the Tribally Controlled Community College Assistance Act, the Indian Education Title of the Education Amendments Act, and the Indian Child Welfare Act (ICWA; Prucha 2000). In 1979 Congress passed the Archaeological Resources Protection Act, and in 1980 the Alaska National Interest Lands Conservation Act (ANILCA; Prucha 2000).[37] But few of these events are attributable to initiatives by Carter or his staff. As of 1975 the policy initiative in Indian affairs had largely shifted to Congress, the topic of the next chapter.

Congress and Indians

Senator James Abourezk

*C*ongressional authority over Indian affairs derives from the commerce clause of Article 1 of the Constitution, which says, "Congress shall have the Power . . . to regulate Commerce with Foreign Nations, and among the several States, and with the Indian Tribes" (Pevar 2002, 58). So long as Indian relations were conducted through treaties, responsibility largely lay with the Senate, which shared with the president the power to make treaties. Largely in response to House objections to this unequal division of labor, treaty making with Indians came to an end in 1871, and henceforth Indian matters were dealt with by both houses, more or less equally (Prucha 1984, 531).

Since the 1820s both houses have had a shifting array of standing and select committees designated to handle Indian affairs in general or specific aspects thereof (Wilkins 1995, 29). Throughout the nineteenth and twentieth centuries, congressmen from the western states with significant Indian populations dominated these committees (McCool 1994, 134). In government reorganization post–World War II, Indian matters in the Senate and in the House were handled by each house's Interior and Insular Affairs Committee (Wilkins 1995, 28). Those were the responsible committees at the time of the passage of the 1975 Indian Self-Determination and Education Assistance Act (Prucha 2000, 275).

By 1977, however, the Senate had created a Select Committee on Indian Affairs, for a two-year term, which kept being temporarily reauthorized until 1984, when it became a permanent committee (Wilkins 1995, 28). The House created a Subcommittee on Indian Affairs and Public Lands in 1977, but it was abolished by 1979, apparently because no one wanted the chairmanship, with Indian matters back to being handled by the entire Interior committee, whose name was changed to Committee on Resources in the 103rd Congress (Wilkins 1995, 28). The chair of the House Interior committee at that time, Mo Udall, seems to have taken on the Indian affairs leadership role (Bee 1992, 145). "'No senior member was willing to handle the post,' said longtime aide Franklin D. Ducheneaux. 'There were too many political headaches and no gain for the senior members, so Mo did it. . . . He was the major influence from 1977 to 1990'" (Carson and Johnson 2001, 204–5).

McCool notes the presence of both pro- and anti-Indian legislators, and "because of the ideological split on the Indian Affairs subcommittees, the subcommittee chair assumed unusual importance. To a certain extent he could orient the subcommittee in an anti-Indian or pro-Indian direction" (1994, 138). Indian matters are of little political mass and are therefore easily moved, even by one determined congressional member (Castile 1992, 170). At one point, this was Henry Jackson, one of the original architects of termination and its supporter well into the seventies, but who sponsored self-determination at the time of its passage in 1975. This switch was clearly linked to an attempt to look presidential during his campaign for that office (Castile 1998b, 105). After his attempt failed in 1976, he seems to have largely lost interest in Indian affairs.

The Indian policy ball at this point passed into very unusual hands, Senator James Abourezk of South Dakota, son of Lebanese migrants who had settled on the Rosebud Reservation. Growing up on and around the reservation, he was one of the few members of Congress with direct personal acquaintance with Indian affairs (Abourezk 1989, 7).[1] His influence was brief: Abourezk served only one term and did not seek reelection; in fact, he claims to have decided not to seek a second term after his first year in the Senate (1989, 4). Abourezk thought, "Whatever power one has as a senator can be used either for oneself or for others, a fact that required me early on [to decide] whether to do something on behalf of the unorganized and the powerless—the Indians, consumers, Palestinians, the poor—or to avoid the controversial position of the advocate, to play it safe, and to try to stay in office forever" (1989, 104).

A disinterest in reelection confers a certain freedom to pursue a political course without reference to its popularity. Despite having the advantage of being a political kamikaze, Abourezk was generally unsuccessful in his attempts to affect most of the policies in which he had a particular interest, notably, United States–Israel–Palestine relations, but in Indian affairs, he made far more of a dent.[2] This is perhaps another illustration of the lack of political weight of Indian affairs, that they can be shifted not only by the interest of one Senator, but also by that of a maverick. Abourezk was appointed chair of the Indian subcommittee of the Interior and Insular Affairs Committee by Henry Jackson, chair of the larger committee, because, Abourezk claims, "no one else wanted the job" (Abourezk 1989, 206).

Other observers have noted the unattractiveness of membership on the Indian committees (McCool 1994, 128; Bee 1982, 81). McCool suggests, "There are two rationales for serving on an Indian affairs committee. The first is based on sympathy for Indians and is primarily moralistic in intent. The second is much more pragmatic; it serves the interests of non-Indians who are either threatened by the actions of the first group—the moralists—or who simply seek to obtain Indian resources, especially land and water" (McCool 1994, 132). An example of the pragmatic was William S. Cohen of Maine: "Cohen, it is important to note, assumed the chairmanship of the committee during the height of eastern Indian land claims. . . . The Maine cases were the leading and potentially most disruptive of these land claims" (Wilkins 1995, 31). Abourezk clearly falls in the moralist category, as Bee notes: "Abourezk was personally interested in Indian affairs . . . his efforts toward improving Indian policy could hardly be dubbed political expediency" (1982, 83).

Abourezk was not impressed by the Carter administration's work for Indians. In his memoirs, *Advise and Dissent,* he notes, "For all his pretense as a liberal, Jimmy Carter did less for American Indians than Richard Nixon. . . . Carter hardly knew that Indians existed" (1989, 205). He also complained of Assistant Secretary Forest Gerard, "nothing happened, despite Gerard's protestations that he would implement recommendations made by the American Indian Policy Review Commission" (1989, 205). Abourezk had a history of disagreement with Gerard dating back to when Gerard served on Senator Henry Jackson's staff. "Scoop Jackson had assigned only one staff member—Forest Gerard—to the Indian subcommittee. Although I was the subcommittee's chairman, Gerard took his orders from Scoop, making the situation both uncomfortable and untenable" (1989, 215).

The American Indian Policy Review Commission

The American Indian Policy Review Commission was a body created by Abourezk in response to what he felt was a lack of support for his subcommittee by Interior Chair Jackson. "I continued to press Scoop for more Indian staff, but to no avail. Bill Van Ness, the Interior Committee's chief council, suggested I try to put together a special commission on Indian problems to get more staff. . . . We appropriated a few million dollars for a two-year study of Indian policy by a body called the American Indian Policy Review Commission, with a mandate to come up with recommendations for both the Congress and the Administration" (Abourezk 1989, 215–16). Prucha suggests, "What Abourezk and his supporters had in mind was a new Merriam report" (1984, 1163).[3]

The proposal was passed by the Senate but its language was much modified by the House: "The strong statements and the pro-Indian tone of the Senate resolution caused consternation among conservative congressmen and threatened a backlash that could destroy the positive features of the proposal, and the House of Representatives, under the leadership of Representative Lloyd Meeds of Washington, considerably moderated the resolution" (Prucha 1984, 1163). With Abourezk as chair, Meeds became the vice chair of the commission, which formed eleven separate task forces, staffed largely with Indians, which heard a wide range of witnesses submit a torrent of policy proposals. The opening statement of the final report notes, "It has been the fortune of this commission to listen attentively to the voice of the Indian rather than the Indian expert. The findings and recommendations which appear in this report are founded on that Indian voice" (AIPRC 1977, 3). The final report, delivered in 1977, tended to endorse all of these voices more or less indiscriminately.

Abourezk notes, "The final commission report, written by the Indian staff members, came out with several hundred recommendations for change, to be implemented by the Administration and Congress. It goes without saying that the recommendations for the Administration were largely ignored" (1989, 217). There were in fact 206 recommendations, ranging from the sweeping "Congress shall enact affirmative legislation to reaffirm and guarantee the permanence and viability of tribal government within the Federal system" (#47) to micro management: "Congress

directs IHS to report on tribal needs for fully equipped ambulances"
(#136). Among the more open-ended injunctions to Congress was that
it move "to provide economic and social programs necessary to raise the
standard of living and social well-being of the Indian people to a level
comparable to the non-Indian society" (#2; AIPRC 1977).

In fairness to the Carter administration, it is difficult to imagine how
any presidents could have managed to put all these ideas into legislation
and push them through Congress. The AIPRC report was certainly not
universally popular; even Lloyd Meeds felt compelled to dissent, complaining of its one-sided advocacy (AIPRC 1977, 571–612). This reaction,
however, may have been due to Meeds, who had been one of the stronger
congressional advocates for Indians, undergoing a dialectical transformation as a result of the fishing-based anti-Indian reaction in his home
state (Bee 1982, 82). After the report, Meeds resigned as chair of the House
Subcommittee on Indian Affairs, which was shortly thereafter abolished
(Officer 1984, 94).

The commission was supposedly attuned to "Indian voices," but
even that was in dispute. Although the staff was heavily Indian, "their appointment was violently criticized by other Indians as not being properly
representative, and the National Congress of American Indians sought
an injunction, unsuccessfully, to prevent the commission's operation on
that ground" (Prucha 1984, 1165). Vine Deloria Jr. notes, "The task forces
quickly politicized both selections to their membership and topics to be
covered, and little of significance was accomplished in the two years the
commission existed" (1984, 128).

Prucha also judges the AIPRC to have been a failure, noting that

> it was caught in the theoretical dilemma that plagued the whole
> movement for self-determination. Although the report was pre-
> mised on the concept of full political sovereignty of the tribes, most
> of the 206 recommendations of the commission were proposals for
> the federal government to appropriate funds for Indian programs
> or in some other way to deliver services to the "sovereign" tribes.
> There was, moreover, such a barrage of demands for funds or other
> congressional and administrative action that it was difficult to know
> where to begin. (Prucha 1984, 1167)

In the end, very few of the recommendations were fulfilled either administratively or legislatively. Both the AIPRC and the Senate select committee called for reorganizing the BIA drastically, particularly to reduce the role of the area offices (Bee 1992, 148); however, as Bee notes, "By 1989—almost fifteen years after they were proposed—these changes had still not been implemented. The area office structure was still intact, although area directors had been removed from line authority in BIA education programs" (1992, 149).

But there was arguably an impact; if nothing else, congressional attention was directed toward Indian affairs. The commission delivered its report in 1977, and in 1978, the small flurry of Indian legislation was surely due at least partly to the issuance of the report. Officer attributes this legislation directly to Abourezk. "The last half of 1978 was a productive time for Indian legislation. Senator Abourezk, who had previously announced his retirement, made the most of his final year in Congress" (Officer 1984, 95). Certainly none of it originated in the Carter White House.

The Indian Child Welfare Act

Of these various pieces of legislation, Abourezk said, "I think that the Indian Child Welfare Act was perhaps the most far-reaching bill that we passed. Prior to the Act's passage, white welfare agencies were working their will on Indian families, much to the detriment of the Indians" (1989, 219). The BIA had in fact pursued a vigorous program of promoting adoption of Indian children by non-Indians since the 1950s termination era, which was drawn to public attention by the Association on American Indian Affairs (Prucha 1984, 1154; Garner 1993). Abourezk held subcommittee hearings on the issue in 1974, and one of the AIPRC task forces did a special study on Indian out-adoption rates, which were increasing, not declining.[4] Legislation was introduced and finally became the Indian Child Welfare Act of 1978 (ICWA), which gave tribes a mediator role in any attempts to adopt the children of their members (Prucha 2000, 294).

The Carter administration did raise some objections: "Some conceivable applications of the bill are probably unconstitutional" and "The bill interferes with a matter which should be left under state jurisdiction." But staff recommended approval, saying, "I believe the bill will be of substantive and symbolic importance to Indians who are justifiably dismayed by the large number of Indian children who are taken from their families and placed in non-Indian homes. A veto of this bill would unnecessarily strain relations with the Indian community."[5] The law has since undergone considerable challenge and clarification in the courts: "The ICWA is now perhaps involved in more litigation than any other Indian statute" (Getches, Wilkinson, and Williams 1998, 660).

American Indian Religious Freedom

Issues of restrictions on Indian religious activity on public lands had been raised in the Nixon era, among other things resulting in the return of Blue Lake to Taos Pueblo (Castile 1998b, 102). Under the stimulus of the AIPRC report and debate, Congress passed a joint resolution August 11, 1978, on American Indian Religious Freedom, which said, "henceforth it shall be the policy of the United States to protect and preserve for American Indians their inherent right of freedom to believe, express and exercise the traditional religions of the American Indian, Eskimo, Aleut, and Native Hawaiians" (Prucha 2000, 289).

Abourezk observed, "The Indian Affairs Committee did manage to pass a couple of worthwhile bills. . . . The Indian Freedom of Religion Act was one. Although it is a Congressional Resolution that has no force of law, it has given the Indians a platform from which to protest the trampling of their religious freedoms by the government" (1989, 219). The major impact of the resolution is to admonish federal agencies to take Indian religious sensibilities into account in their decision making. Mo Udall, during the debate, said, "All this simple resolution says to the Forest Service, to the Park Service, to the managers of public lands is that if there is a place where Indians traditionally congregate to hold one of their rites and ceremonies, let them come on unless there is some overriding reason why they should not" (Getches, Wilkinson, and Williams 1998, 766). Similarly, Carter aide Eizenstat said, "The resolution is designed primarily to assure that Federal Programs (such as Federal land management and customs procedures) are administered to accommodate and be sensitive to traditional native religious beliefs and practices."[6]

The Archaeological Resources Protection Act

One significant piece of legislation related to Indians in this same flurry did not originate with Abourezk or his committee: the Archaeological Resources Protection Act of 1979 (Prucha 2000, 295). Although such antiquities in the continental United States are obviously mostly those of American Indian cultures, it was an archaeologist's bill, not an Indian bill per se, but it did include language requiring for the first time consultation with tribal governments regarding antiquities on reservations (Prucha 2000, 296).[7]

The existing Antiquities Act of 1906, which protected archaeological remains on public lands, was tested in the courts in 1974 and 1977 and found unconstitutionally vague, and it was in any case toothless (Collins and Michel 1985, 85; Cheek 1991, 33). Subsequently, a group of concerned archaeologists and the Society of American Archaeology began an effort to get new and stronger legislation to protect archaeological sites from looters. After futile efforts to work through Interior, they drew up their own draft and persuaded Mo Udall to introduce it (Collins and Michel 1985; Cheek 1991).

Although Udall was supportive of the new legislation, there was a problem with early draft provisions specifically repudiating the 1906 act. Udall had waged an unsuccessful effort to pass legislation protecting Alaskan wilderness lands, and President Carter then used the provisions of the Antiquities Act to withdraw seventeen parcels as national monuments (Collins and Michel 1985, 88; Carson and Johnson 2001, 198). Presidents from Theodore Roosevelt on have used the act in this way, and the final version of the new bill left out repudiation of the old bill, leaving this mechanism intact.[8] Although Abourezk was the more spectacular champion of the Indian, Udall was the more persistent. His biographers note of his Indian bills, "from his position as chairman of the Interior Committee, Mo guided 184 bills through the Congress, many of them individual efforts to help just one of the more than 500 tribes" (Carson and Johnson 2001, 203).

The Tribally Controlled Community College Assistance Act

The first Indian-controlled community college was established at Many Farms on the Navajo reservation in 1969. It was a direct spinoff of the OEO-sponsored experiment in Indian education established at nearby Rough Rock (Castile 1968; 1998b, 108). Community colleges are generally state funded, but the newly emerging Indian colleges were to become almost entirely federally funded. The tribes possess the power to tax their own members and the enterprises of nonmembers on their reservations, so they are seemingly capable of supporting their own education systems as do states and local polities (Pevar 2002, 204). Unfortunately, most Indian reservations are economically depressed and incapable of internally sustaining high levels of taxation for education, hence the dependency on federal funding. Congress had recognized this need in the Navajo Community College Act of 1971 (Castile 1998b, 108).

As more such colleges began to emerge on other reservations, Congress acted in 1978 to extend similar funding to them in the Tribally Controlled Community College Assistance Act (Prucha 1984, 1147; Prucha 2000, 291). The Carter staff had some objections, primarily in relation to funding levels, but recommended its approval: "While this is not an ideal bill, its cost is not great, the Indian constituency is a sympathetic one, and Representative Blouin, its sponsor, has been helpful."[9]

There was some other activity regarding Indian education in this same period, also not emanating from the Indian committees per se. Robert Kennedy in 1967 chaired a special subcommittee, on Indian Education, of the Committee on Labor and Public Welfare (Castile 1998b, 63). In 1978 the House Committee on Education and Labor similarly appointed a Special Advisory Study Group on Indian Education (Prucha 1984, 1145). Both reports found much fault with the BIA administration of Indian education, and in both cases the end result was the insertion of Indian education titles in the more general education amendment acts of 1972 and 1978 (Castile 1998b, 107; Prucha 1984, 1145). The 1978 amendments directed BIA to draw up standards and to some limited extent reorganized the administration of Indian education (Prucha 2000, 292).

Federal Acknowledgment

Although Abourezk thought the ICWA was his most important accomplishment, arguably the Federal Acknowledgment Process, which he stimulated, is more significant. Although retention of their children, as addressed by the ICWA, is fundamental to the survival of Indian groups, perhaps even more fundamental is the question of whether the group exists at all—as Indians. As the government-to-government status of Indians improved under the self-determination policy, more groups began to find it worthwhile to seek recognition or re-recognition as Indian tribes. One of the issues that the AIPRC then addressed was the question of federal recognition or acknowledgment of such Indian groups.

Throughout most of the history of federal-Indian relations, this was done on an ad hoc basis. Those "recognized" as tribes were simply those with whom the government had some formal dealings, most commonly through treaties (Quinn 1990). The native peoples' aboriginal political organization ranged from familistic bands, tribes, and chiefdoms to small conquest empires, but all eventually came to be called "tribes." The definition of a tribe is de facto, "native group with formal relations with the federal government," since it has no reference to the actual internal social organization of the peoples so labeled.[10] In many cases "tribes" were simply created by fiat for treaty purposes, calling all those occupying a specific area covered by a treaty a single tribe, although as in the case of the Yakima treaty, for example, some thirteen distinct peoples were subsumed (Prucha 1994, 212).

It was not until the Indian Reorganization Act in 1934 that a single set of rules was drawn up defining those who qualified for organization under that act. Using these criteria, the Collier administration created the first list of 258 "recognized" tribes (Beinart 1999, 35; Miller 2004, 28; Quinn 1990, 357). Felix Cohen, in his *Handbook of Federal Indian Law*, set out the criteria the BIA had developed at that time for determining "tribal existence":

(1) That the group has had treaty relations with the United States. (2) That the group has been denominated a tribe by Act of Congress or Executive order. (3) That the group has been treated as having collective rights in tribal lands or funds, even though not expressly

designated a tribe. (4) That the group has been treated as a tribe or band by other Indian tribes. (5) That the group has exercised political authority over its members, through a tribal council or other forms. (1942, 271)

Following these guidelines, until the seventies the BIA was the primary judge of who was an Indian tribe, although some tribes sought and gained recognition by special legislation.

In the seventies a number of problems arose as "unrecognized" Indian groups gained court victories in Washington over fishing rights and in New England over land claims (Prucha 1984, 1195). William W. Quinn Jr. notes, "As useful as the Final Report of the American Indian Policy Review Commission was it was not as persuasive as a series of judicial decisions in the mid-seventies in motivating the Department of the Interior to adopt a uniform procedure and standard criteria for recognizing unrecognized Indian tribes" (1990, 362). The Abourezk report might have been more important than Quinn suggests, however, since it took a strong position favoring a sweeping opening up of federal recognition to over 100,000 people in 133 groups (Beinart 1999, 36; Miller 2004, 39). The report recommended that "Congress adopt, in a concurrent resolution, a statement of policy affirming its intention to recognize all Indian tribes as eligible for the benefits and protections of general Indian legislation and Indian policy" (AIPRC 1977, 480).

This potential expansion of recognition to all who asked for it obviously raised serious questions for both the bureau and the existing tribes (Miller 2004, 41). Bee notes that there was considerable debate, with the already established tribes and the NCAI among the strongest opponents of increased recognition, because they feared dilution of federal funding (1982, 111). Federal funding did in fact remain basically constant as the number of tribes qualified to receive it increased in this period.

Prucha notes, "Some government action was needed that would satisfy all parties. A move was made for congressional action by introduction of a bill in the Senate on December 15, 1977, and another in the House on May 11, 1978, to establish administrative procedures and guidelines for the secretary of the interior in acknowledging tribes, but the goal was accomplished instead by administrative action" (1984, 1195). The bureau in 1977 drew up a proposed list of procedures, and "the draft became a target for others to shoot at, but also a base from which to work to draft new regulations" (Bee 1982, 114).

The NCAI, the harshest critic, was induced to hold national meetings to suggest changes to the draft, and in the end it approved the idea of new recognition procedures with few specifics (Bee 1982, 115). The final version did not in fact address the principal NCAI concern over diluted funding. "There was nothing . . . to ensure that funds for the newly recognized groups would not dip into monies appropriated for already recognized tribes or existing programs" (Bee 1982, 115). The procedures were codified (25 *U.S.C.* 54), saying, "The purpose of this part is to establish a departmental procedure and policy for acknowledging that certain American Indian tribes exist" and limiting the possible applicants by saying, "This part is intended to cover only those American Indian groups indigenous to the continental United States which are ethnically and culturally identifiable" (Prucha 2000, 290).

Applicants for federal status would have to petition for recognition and in so doing satisfy several basic criteria.

> Evidence to be relied upon . . . shall include one or more of the following: (1) Repeated identification by Federal authorities; (2) Longstanding relationships with State governments based on identification of the group as Indian; (3) Repeated dealings with a county, parish, or other local government in a relationship based on the group's Indian identity; (4) Identification as an Indian entity by records in courthouses, churches or schools; (5) Identification as an Indian entity by anthropologists, historians or other scholars; (6) Repeated identification as an Indian entity in newspapers or books; (7) Repeated identification and dealings as an Indian entity with recognized Indian tribes or national Indian organizations. (Prucha 2000, 290)

The workings of this procedure have turned out to be slow, with very few new tribes qualifying under its provisions. Of over two hundred petitions made since 1978, by 2000, only thirty-four had been resolved by the Branch of Acknowledgment and Research (BAR) process—fifteen recognized, nineteen not (Miller 2004, 54).

Some previously terminated groups had no choice but to pursue legislation since the 1978 recognition procedure specifically excludes groups that are "the subject of congressional legislation which has expressly terminated or forbidden the Federal relationship" (Prucha 2000, 291). Beginning with the Menominee Restoration Act in 1973, terminated groups have had to achieve re-recognition by special congressional legislation (Castile 1998b, 148). During the Carter years, the Siletz of Oregon persuaded Congress to pass the Siletz Restoration Act in 1977, and a reservation was established for them in 1980 (NARF 2000, 3). Carter's signing statement again stressed his theme of settlement of Indian claims through negotiation, saying the bill "reflects this administration's plan and strikes a balance among the interests of the tribe and those of the local community, the State of Oregon, and the Federal government."[11]

The Pascua Yaqui

Even as the new recognition procedure was being debated, and subsequent to its establishment, some groups still preferred to pursue recognition through special legislation. Given Congress's plenary authority over Indian affairs, in the end, who is or is not to be recognized as an Indian tribe is entirely up to Congress, regardless of any guidelines pursued by the BIA branch of acknowledgement. A case in point are the Pascua Yaqui of Tucson, Arizona, who began to seek recognition in 1976 and finally achieved it on September 18, 1978, by special legislation (Castile 2002).[12]

The Yaqui are an indigenous people of Mexico, whose prehistoric homeland is along the Rio Yaqui in Sonora, some 600 kilometers from the United States border. Fleeing persecution in their homeland, a few arrived in the United States in the 1880s: "These few were augmented just after 1900 by hundreds more seeking to escape deportation. From 1900 to 1910 perhaps 60 percent of all Yaquis who ever came to the United States entered, that is to say probably about 1000—a new wave of migration came in 1916–1917—those who came about 1907 and about 1917 constituted a nucleus who settled permanently and founded the Arizona Yaqui communities" (Spicer 1980, 236–37). In Tucson in 1921, some Yaqui established a community that they called Pascua (Spicer 1940, 25).

In 1963, with the help of Mo Udall, these Yaqui successfully sought and acquired a tract of federal land to establish New Pascua (Castile 1998b, 35). Udall introduced a private bill and wrote to Wayne Aspinall, chair of the House Committee on Interior and Insular Affairs, to schedule hearings: "In this bill I am asking for a simple grant of land for a group of Mexican Indians who arrived in this country too late to receive recognition by the Bureau of Indian Affairs. I am not asking that this tribe be accorded any status as a ward of the federal government."[13] Passed as Private Law 88-350, Section 4 of the act states, "Nothing in this Act shall make such Yaqui Indians eligible for any services performed by the United States for Indians because of their status as Indians, and none of the statutes of the United States which affect Indians because of their status as Indians shall be applicable to the Yaqui Indians."[14]

Although not officially Indians, the Yaqui were undeniably poor and were able to persuade the OEO to support a community development project on their new land from 1966 to 1969 (Castile 1998b, 35). As the community grew, some Yaqui leaders began to consider the possible advantages of becoming a recognized tribe and went again to Mo Udall for support. Udall, as chair of the Interior and Insular Committee, introduced a bill in the House on April 25, 1977, "To provide for the extension of certain Federal benefits, services, and assistance to the Pascua Yaqui Indians of Arizona, and for other purposes."[15] Senator Abourezk and Arizona Senator Dennis DeConcini introduced a companion bill on April 25, 1977.[16]

Forest Gerard, assistant secretary of Interior for Indian affairs, argued against enactment at the hearings, suggesting instead that the Yaqui apply under the already proposed new rules of acknowledgement. "We believe that the Pascua Yaqui should be afforded the same opportunity to apply for the extension of benefits and services as any other group of Indians seeking such services."[17] The sponsors of the bill, however, pressed ahead with its consideration, presumably because it was unlikely the Yaqui would qualify under the formal guidelines. One of the principal difficulties was the nonindigenous status of the Yaqui.

Senator Abourezk adopted language at the hearings to assert Yaqui aboriginality, based on material that had been submitted to the AIPRC: "The Yaqui Indians are descendents of the ancient Toltecs who ranged from what is now the city of Durango, north to Southern Colorado, and west to California. The U.S. boundary line, determined by agreement with Mexico, divided the Indian territóries occupied by Pimas, Papagos, Apaches, Yaquis and other Indians."[18] Senator DeConcini had inserted the same Toltec language into the *Congressional Record* as well as asserting, "Ruins of communities built by the ancestors of the Yaquis and other Pueblo Indians are found in New Mexico and other areas of the Southwest."[19] This view, entirely unsupported by archaeological evidence, was apparently accepted since the bill was passed and sent on to President Carter.

OMB argued against Carter's approval: "The available evidence indicates they are not a group of Indians indigenous to the United States, did not have an aboriginal range in what is now the United States, and have not had a continuous tribal existence on lands that are now within the United States." They expressed concern that "Your approval of S.1633 could arguably establish a precedent for recognizing other Indian groups which do not meet the current criteria for Federal recognition." In the end they acquiesced: "We recommend that you approve S.1633, but believe that such action should be accompanied by a memo from you to Secretary Andrus which makes plain that your approval of S.1633 is not to be taken as a precedent for recognizing such groups, and that you expect the Department to rigorously apply their new administrative criteria to such groups."[20]

White House domestic policy staff prepared an advisory statement for the president, recommending his approval. In a section "Arguments for Veto," they say only, "The Yaqui do not qualify under administrative criteria for tribal recognition, and this legislation might be viewed as a precedent for other groups." In the section "Arguments for Signing," they resolve the objection: "Justice feels that this legislation will not create an adverse legal precedent applicable to Indian claims cases, an earlier OMB concern." The only positive argument is simply, "This bill is important to Congressman Udall, who sponsored it in the house. He feels very strongly about this bill."[21] Udall had been a serious rival to Carter for the Democratic nomination in 1976 and was now a senior and influential representative. As with other Indian issues, in the end the approval of Yaqui recognition seems to have boiled down to the will of one determined congressman.

The Self-Determination Process?

Among other issues that Abourezk's committee looked into was the progress of contracting under the Indian self-determination policy; oversight
hearings were held for that purpose (Prucha 1984, 1161).[22] Abourezk also
requested that the General Accounting Office (GAO) look into the progress of the process, which they did with five tribal examples, issuing a report, *The Indian Self-Determination Act: Many Obstacles Remain.*[23] The
GAO report was moderate, but the general tone of Indian spokespersons
at the hearings was remarkably negative, mostly aimed at BIA handling of
the contracting procedures (McClellan 1990, 50). The program had been
in operation for only two years, and "both the tribes and the agency personnel needed time to unravel the snarls in the system. What bothered the
Indians was the suspicion that the difficulties were not temporary at all
but were instead symptomatic of a long-standing fundamental incompetence among bureaucrats" (Bee 1982, 97).

Responding to the Indians' complaints, Abourezk proposed to amend
the act, primarily to allow for block grants, which had been a Nixon aim.
"The proposal would make it possible for Indian tribes to obtain a single
block grant for multifaceted tribal programs replacing existing BIA or
IHS services or for new programs the tribes might design" (Bee 1982, 99).
In the hearings, there was some Indian support for the plan, but generally, the federal agencies involved were not supportive, and the bill died
in committee (Bee 1982, 103).[24] The bureau continued to review tribal
contracts piecemeal, and while slow, progress was in fact being made.

Prucha notes, "Despite the strong rhetoric of Indian leaders about
the failure of the act to provide genuine self-determination, in fact a large
number of contracts were concluded under its provisions. In fiscal year
1980, 370 tribes contracted for the operation of $200 million worth of
programs under the Indian Self-Determination Act, and 22.3 million was
paid to the tribes to cover their overhead in the contracts" (1984, 1162).
By the end of the Carter administration, Indian self-determination was
still the prevailing policy, and despite a great deal of growing pains, progress in that direction seemed to be made through contracting. Despite
Abourezk's efforts and that of his committee, no fundamental change of
direction emerged.

The Last Mile

American Indian activism, at least the flamboyant variant represented by the American Indian Movement (AIM), first grabbed national media attention with the occupation of Alcatraz Island in 1969 and reached a high point of publicity with the occupation of Wounded Knee in 1973. There is a considerable literature on the rise and fall of this Indian social movement, almost all of it concentrated on the peak years 1969–1973 (Castile 1998b, ch. 5; Barringer 1997; Hertzberg 1988; T. Johnson 1996; Smith and Warrior 1996). The movement survived beyond this period, but after Wounded Knee, the media appear to have largely lost interest. One author called the demonstrations "actorvism," and in the Carter administration, there was a final bit of theater in the form of a march on Washington in 1978, billed as the Longest Walk (Prucha 1994, 424; Stripes 1999). Some accounts of AIM use this event as the marker date of its final decline from national prominence (Baylor 1994; Johnson, Nagel, and Champagne 1997).

   This demonstration was ostensibly in response to a "backlash" of anti-Indian sentiment in Congress (Nagel 1997, 175; Nichols 2003, 207; Prucha 1994, 422; T. Taylor 1983, 42). Much of this originated in Washington State, where Slade Gorton, as attorney general, parlayed opposition to Indian fishing rights into a place in the Senate (Castile 1985). In 1977 John E. Cunningham of Washington, similarly elected by opposition to Indian fishing rights, introduced the Native American Equal Opportunity Act, which "would have unilaterally abrogated all Indian treaties, broken up Indian communal assets, and terminated the special services guaranteed to Indians" (Prucha 1994, 423). Lloyd Meeds, also of Washington, once pro-Indian, also succumbed to home-state sentiments and introduced legislation. "His bill would have weakened tribal powers by extending state and local jurisdiction over tribal lands and other resources and would have limited Indian rights to water" (Prucha 1994, 424).[25]

   Neither of these bills ever had a chance of enactment, being too far out of the prevailing mood of support for minority rights. "None of the backlash bills passed the 95th Congress. In the House they all died in committee, with a singular lack of energy being expended on their behalf by those who introduced them" (Bee 1982, 149). In retrospect it seems clear they were largely introduced for home-state consumption, with no expectation by their sponsors that they would ever pass into law (Bee 1982, 151). But at the time, just their introduction was worrisome to Indian leaders and their friends. The NCAI and the NTCA organized a United Effort Trust to confront these bills and to cooperate with the more radical efforts of AIM (Bee 1982, 147).

A handful of AIM members and some other advocates set out to march from California to Washington. The Longest Walk, when it arrived in Washington five months later in July, issued a fourteen-page "manifesto," inserted into the *Congressional Record* by Abourezk but receiving no serious attention from the administration.[26] The group, swelled by supporters to approximately 2,800, camped for a week to dramatize their demands.[27] Dennis Banks had written to request a meeting with the president, and the vice president did meet with representatives of the group.[28] Although the president never actually met with them, his staff had prepared remarks for a possible "drop by" visit. These contained a warning not to accept or comment upon the manifesto: "A formal response might present unnecessary difficulties both domestically and internationally."[29]

The backlash debates and the Longest Walk demonstration may perhaps have contributed to the skittish Carter administration's decision simply to avoid issuing any Indian policy statement whatever.[30] But Bee suggests, "The Indian advocates' activities . . . were not primarily responsible for stifling whatever congressional backlash effort existed. They developed too late, after the bills had already been pronounced dead by key members of Congress" (1982, 149). Subsequently, AIM lost the eye of the media and faded from the national scene except for occasional newsworthy actions, as when Russell Means ran for vice president on the ticket of Larry Flynt (Means 1995, 442; Smith and Warrior 1996, 278).

Less Is More
The Reagan Administration

*R*onald Reagan succeeded Jimmy Carter, and the considerable literature on the Reagan presidency includes some consideration of his impact on Indian affairs (Castile 1998a; Cook 1994, 1996; Esber 1992; Hanson 2001; Hertzberg 1982; Jorgensen 1986; Manning 2001; C. Morris 1988; Olson and Deer 1982; Stull 1990; Stull, Schultz, and Cadue 1986). President Reagan was certainly far more familiar with Indians than Carter was—albeit imaginary ones. This is evident in comments Reagan made while attending a summit meeting in Moscow in 1988. Asked a question by reporters about American Indians who wanted to meet with him, he responded:

> Let me tell you just a little something about the American Indian in our land. We have provided millions of acres of land for what are called preservations—or reservations, I should say. They, from the beginning, announced that they wanted to maintain their way of life, as they had always lived there in the desert and the plains and so forth. And we set up these reservations so they could, and have a Bureau of Indian Affairs to help take care of them. . . . And they're free to leave the reservations and be American citizens among the rest of us, and many do. Some still prefer, however, that way—that early way of life. And we've done everything we can to meet their demands as to how they wanted to live. Maybe we made a mistake. Maybe we should not have humored them in that wanting to stay in that kind of primitive lifestyle. Maybe we should have said, no, come join us; be citizens along with the rest of us. . . . Some of them became very wealthy because some of those reservations were overlaying great pools of oil, and you can get very rich pumping oil. And so, I don't know what their complaint might be.[1]

The style of this comment is a reflection of President Reagan's general habit of explanation by anecdote, based on fanciful history, often derived from the movies (Cannon 1991, 58; Fireman 1995; Slotkin 1992, 643; Vaughn 1994). One biographer noted, "He spoke in symbolic terms of a vision of the future rooted in the American past—but a cleaned up Disneyland kind of past, free of a dark side of poverty-blighted dreams, racial oppression or imperialistic wars" (Pemberton 1997, 204). Regarding the place of Indians in this vision, Hazel W. Hertzberg has commented, "in the Reagan happy hunting ground, the tribes are eternally filled with the entrepreneurial spirit. Using their own native materials, guided by the principles of free enterprise, and financed by a mixture of tribal and private free investment, they design, manufacture and distribute their own fringed, beaded safety net. That's how Mr. Reagan sees it. But then he was always the cowboy, never the Indian" (1982, 18).[2]

His manipulation of Indian reality for non-Indian symbolic purposes is of course not unique to Reagan but epidemic in American history (Castile 1996). As California governor, he did have an active role in blocking the Dos Rios Dam, which would have flooded the ancestral lands of the Yuki Indians, but Reagan had little else to do personally with Indian affairs either as governor or as president (Cannon 2003, 310–13). In his autobiography (1990) he takes no note of American Indians, and the works of his major biographers mention them passingly, if at all (Cannon 1982, 349; Cannon 1991, 530; Cannon 2003, 51, 310–13; Pemberton 1997; N. Reagan 1989; Strober and Strober 1998).[3] Those on the White House staff who were concerned with Indian affairs complained of an inability to schedule meetings for Indian leaders with Reagan and of his slow action on Indian policy they devised for him.[4] One commented, "With his term half over, the President has never been within hand shaking distance of an Indian leader."[5]

While he may not have had much personal interest in Indians, Indian policy has always reflected large-scale social policies, and there Reagan did have "a handful of bedrock convictions" (Cannon 1991, 55; Castile 1992, 171). He left the details to his staff, but on his behalf, staff members pursued these basic themes in all areas, including Indian policy. He announced them to Congress early on: "First we must cut the growth of government spending. Second, we must cut tax rates so that once again work will be rewarded and savings encouraged. Third, we must carefully remove the tentacles of excessive government regulation which are strangling our economy" (Rayack 1987, 173).

Reagan was not just trying to save money by cutting federal programs but thought that many social programs were inherently harmful, an idea shared with his guru of supply-side economics, Milton Friedman (Rayack 1987). Reagan noted, "I'm trying to undo the 'Great Society.' It was LBJ's war on poverty that led us to our present mess" (Pemberton 1997, 208). Reagan also observed, "Government does not solve problems, it subsidizes them" and declared his intention of "getting government out of the way of the people" (Cannon 1991, 20, 90).

How did this translate into Indian affairs? The self-determination policy inaugurated in 1975 was very much about getting the federal government out of the way of the Indian people and would thus fit nicely into the Reagan program. Deriving directly from the LBJ Great Society programs, however, was self-determination to be undone? In fact, self-determination had been made palatable by being transmogrified in the Nixon administration from a Great Society program to a form of Nixonian New Federalism, which now could become part of the Reagan New Federalism (Conlan 1988, 110; Jorgensen 1986; Williamson 1990).

Self-determination policy by 1980 had taken on a kind of momentum, and in the campaign, the Reagan staff announced its commitment to it, stressing its Republican origins. "I endorse 'Indian self-determination' as national policy. The Indian Self-Determination Act was proposed by a Republican administration and enacted by Congress to provide the legal and administrative vehicle for the tribal governments to secure control and management of Federal programs designed to serve their constituencies" (Reagan 1980, 7). Once Reagan was in office, a White House working group on Indian policy, chaired by Kenneth L. Smith, the Reagan assistant secretary for Indian affairs, was formed in 1982, but a presidential policy statement prepared by that group did not appear until 1983.[6]

Reagan appointed James G. Watt as secretary of the interior and Kenneth L. Smith as assistant secretary for Indian affairs. Watt, a remarkably outspoken man for a political appointee, quickly ran into conflict with environmentalists and later with the Indians (Cawley 1986). Smith, a Warm Springs Wascoe, had had considerable success in promoting economic development on that reservation and was selected to pursue such development throughout Indian country (Cook 1996, 14; C. Morris 1988, 732). Both officials were committed to the administration's general policy principals, including the focus on cutting government programs and costs while promoting economic enterprise. True to the administration's promises, the Reagan budget proposals for 1982 set out to cut government spending, including Indian programs (C. Morris 1988, 733).

Less Is More

Almost immediately, various Indian representatives expressed their dismay and displeasure with the proposed budget cuts. Responding to the Papago chair's protests, a BIA official noted that the cuts for the overall bureau budget amounted to $75,961,000 but also indicated that the vast majority would be absorbed by the BIA central and area offices, not the local programs. "The proposed plan applies as much of the reduction to Bureau overhead as possible."[7] Smith also suggested, "You can be assured that in proposing any further BIA reductions we intend to adhere to the philosophy and principles established under the Indian Self-Determination policy and we will continue to respect and maintain the program priorities established by tribes. To this end we intend to absorb as much of any proposed reductions as possible at the Central and Area office levels."[8]

The Reagan staff also explained that these cuts were only the Indians' fair share of the more general federal belt tightening. Smith, for example, told the NCAI, "all of us here would like these budget cuts to come in programs other than the Indian programs—but if we are realistic and reasonable we have to expect to share in some of the cuts."[9] While this makes superficial sense, in fact the impact of the cuts in federal spending on the reservations was much greater than that of the cuts for the nation as a whole (Hertzberg 1982).

One source estimates six times greater, because the reservations were vastly more dependent on federal funds than typical American communities were (White 1991, 608). For example, in 1982, the first year of Reagan budgeting, the Kickapoo Tribe's budget was cut by two thirds, and Navajo unemployment went from a pre-Reagan rate of 38 percent to

72 percent (Stull, Schultz, and Cadue 1986, 49; Hertzberg 1982, 17). One Reagan White House staff member commented on the Navajo situation and the complaints of its chair, Peter MacDonald: "MacDonald's concern now is Indian unemployment, which has gone from 40 percent to 75 percent in the past year, largely because their 'employment' was through programs like CETA which have been ended or reduced by this administration."[10] It was not just the CETA cuts that created problems. As Bee noted for the Quechuan, "At Fort Yuma, as on many reservations, virtually all the local jobs come from tribal or federal government programs" (Bee 1990, 59; Novack 1990, 639). The tribal governmental jobs and programs are themselves generally dependent on federal funds.

Some argued that the funding and services supplied to reservation peoples could not be cut in the same fashion as general government programs because they are treaty obligations (Esber 1992, 214). For example, NTCA president Wendell Chino wrote of the Reagan cuts and the goal of self-sufficiency, "In order to be economically self-sufficient we must continue to receive aid to educate and train our people, to plan and implement economic development programs, and to help support our governments and provide basic services to our people in the interim, all guaranteed by treaty."[11] Of such frequent resort to treaty rhetoric, Prucha has commented, "Anything an Indian group wanted could be said to be provided 'in the treaties.' Conversely, every evil encountered could be blamed on the 'broken treaties'" (1994, 410).

In general, the Reagan administration treated Indian programs as line items in a federal budget, subject to the federal budgetary process like any other. They explicitly resisted and limited recognition of trust obligations. Reagan vetoed a bill to give support to tribally controlled community colleges, saying, "College level Indian education has never been characterized by law or treaty as a trust responsibility for the Federal government."[12] Shortly thereafter, he vetoed a bill regarding general Indian education, saying, "The provision of Federal education assistance to Indian students is not characterized in law or treaty as a trust responsibility, and has not been held by courts to be so."[13]

The leaders and lobbyists who might have clarified the Indians' unique budgetary situation unfortunately tended to express themselves in impolitic terms. Chino, for example, declared in a letter to Reagan,

"To date your administration has failed miserably in your stated objectives. . . . The budget cuts as proposed . . . will destroy the progress we have made to date and reduce our tribal peoples to welfare status."[14] The Reagan White House staff seemed taken aback by the hostile tone of the NTCA memo, which also complained of failure to meet with NTCA and demanded the resignation of the secretary of the interior. One Reagan staff member commented, "It is clear that many Indian leaders have a serious lack of political sensitivity. We will continue to work with responsible Indian leadership, particularly tribal governments."[15] NTCA, which had been formed in 1971 with the support of the Nixon administration, lost its federal funding in 1986, in part because of its poor relations with the administration (Castile 1998b, 86; Cook 1996, 19; Jorgensen 1986, 11).

The venerable NCAI appears to have been in better favor. Reagan presidential advisor Elizabeth Dole suggested in 1983 that the NCAI "are supportive of our policy initiative and have a very healthy, open relationship with this administration." Ron Andrade, executive director of NCAI, was characterized as "the best staffer in the Indian organization community."[16] It is very doubtful that the NCAI supported large-scale budget cuts, but few protests by them exist in the Reagan papers. NCAI, never dependent on federal funds, soldiered on as the principal Indian lobbying group after the fall of NTCA.

Kenneth Smith replied on the president's behalf to the NTCA memo

Although it was not possible to exempt Federal programs serving Indians from the budget reductions announced March 10, . . . this administration intends to build upon the self-determination policy initiated by the 1970 Presidential Message on Indian Affairs. A primary concern will be the development of tribal self-sufficiency to the greatest extent possible to reduce dependency on Federal staff and funds with its associated interference in tribal affairs. Further we shall continue to fulfill our treaty and trust responsibilities.[17]

In 1982, some tax relief was provided to the tribes. Congress passed the Indian Tribal Governmental Status Act, which "provides them a favorable tax status, similar to states and local government for federal tax purposes" (Getches, Wilkinson, and Williams 1998, 684).

Still, OMB proposed further cuts in October, which drew still more protest from NTCA, including a "demonstration."[18] This, in fact, involved only a handful of people, and "According to Ron Andrade, Executive Director of the National Congress of American Indians, this was a typically ill organized Elmer Savilla effort. Most tribal chairmen received word of the demonstration only a few days in advance . . . there was no specific relationship between the visit to the hill and the current legislative schedule. . . . About the only positive comments they had were those regarding the administration's block grant program. The delegations ran the gamut from polite to enraged."[19]

Elmer M. Savilla, executive director of NTCA, at this point wrote and asked that Reagan "effectuate less stringent cuts which would reflect, within the Department of the Interior, a regard for Indians as a people with legal entitlements and needs as opposed to the other Interior Departments, who only deal with impersonal resources."[20] Savilla also wrote in a sarcastic tone to one of the president's staff: "I am sure that President Reagan has tried to get in touch with us to answer our many letters and telephone messages but they have not been getting through to us. I would not want the American Indian people to think that empty promises have been made. . . . I am sure that . . . the Indian programs are being cut for our own good. After all who needs a 'safety net' when we have you all. Thanks a bunch." Special assistant Morton C. Blackwell responded, "Let me say that I was surprised that you would direct a letter of such tone to Mr. Carleson, who above all the others, is the principal fighter in the ongoing fight for meaningful block grants to tribe governments."[21]

As the cost cutting proceeded, the administration made proposals that amounted to the "block grants" that had been unsuccessfully sought by Abourezk and Nixon. "This new initiative intends to move towards providing a single grant to each tribe for any number of the consolidated Bureau programs it may wish to operate."[22] Initially, it would not be applicable to all tribes. "Consistent with the President's program, the Bureau is initiating the Consolidated Tribal Government Program as a pilot or (prototype) project this fiscal year. The CTGP will allow tribal governments to cluster a number of similar programs or services under a single contract. The tribes will determine their own needs and priorities and plan and implement programs to meet their particular needs and priorities under CTGP."[23]

The bureau did in fact attempt to keep the cuts focused on the over-head and not the local programs. "To the credit of the Reagan adminis-tration, one area in which BIA appropriations increased was that of tribal contracts through the Indian Self-Determination and Assistance Act of 1975 . . . for the tribal administration of Federal services. . . . In 1980, tribes were contracting $203 million in federal programs, and by 1984, that amount had risen to $315 million" (Cook 1996, 19). The adminis-tration, stingy with money, could be generous with symbols, as in the proclamation by Reagan of May 13, 1983, as "American Indian Day," and in 1986, upping the ante to a whole week.[24]

The Indian Policy Message

While the dialogue over budget cutting was going on, the administration was preparing a presidential message on Indian policy. The administra-tion had created an Indian affairs working group in August 1981 to review policy and prepare a policy statement. This was chaired by Kenneth Smith, with Morton Blackwell, special assistant to the president, and Lo Anne Wagner, special assistant to the deputy assistant to the president for pol-icy development, as the principal White House participants.[25] John Mc-Claughry, also of the Office for Policy Development, was a rather skeptical contributor.

By his own admission inexperienced in Indian policy, McClaughry thought radical change was needed: "The only way we can escape the trap we are facing is to design a radically new Indian policy, based on maximum self-determination for the tribes, and the massive reduction of the Federal service bureaucracies which now eat up a lot of Indian money."[26] But he did not think the working group was prepared to make such profound changes. "I do not have the feeling that Smith is very keen on doing anything more than going through the motions. . . . Smith an-nounced that this working group would not deal with the really major Indian questions—land and water. . . . In short, I am apprehensive about getting a product out of this group."[27]

An initial draft was prepared by May 1982, and comments were so-licited from Indians. "We have asked the National Congress of American Indians, National Tribal Chairman's Association, and Republican Indian

Federation (part of the RNC) to submit suggestions and recommendations from their membership and tribes no later than May 28."[28] In August 1982, the draft policy statement was submitted by the working group for review by the Cabinet Council on Human Resources.[29] Of that report's emphasis, Smith said, "The Working Group chose to focus the statement on the two basic policy areas of encouraging self-government and the development of reservation economies."[30]

There was a considerable delay after the completion of this draft in August; the president did not deliver it as an Indian policy message until January 24, 1983. This appears to have been largely a matter of fitting it into the presidential schedule, but the delay triggered a curious internal White House staff debate over the "Indian vote." One staff member urged that the president issue the message soon because "the votes of reservation Indians could be a swing factor in several Western races."[31] Another noted that a South Dakota Republican Representative, Clint Roberts, had made "campaign comments to the effect that reservations should be terminated" and that this needed to be counteracted. "It is no exaggeration to say that if we issue the statement soon we may garner 100,000 to 150,000 Indian votes we might not otherwise get."[32] Several other staff memos supported this view. "It is the joint assessment of Bob Carleson and Ed Rollins that, if we issue the statement prior to the election, we may well garner 100,000 to 150,000 Indian votes we may not otherwise get."[33]

The report was not issued until after the elections, and what is curious about the debate is the amount of staff concern over the miniscule amount of votes at stake, roughly those of Walla Walla County. Just as no politician kisses babies with the baby vote in mind, Indian policy is also often a symbolic gesture, aimed at impressing other, larger constituencies. (Castile 1992, 178) The Nixon administration, for example, promoted the self-determination policy "to show more heart" to numerically larger minority populations and their supporters, not to court the tiny Indian vote spread over many states (Castile 1998b, 76).

The Reagan staffers may have developed an exaggerated idea of the Indian constituency from the results of the 1980 census, which showed growth of the Indian population from 792,730 in 1970 to 1,534,000 in 1980. This growth was not possible by natural increase and was the result of the census policy of unchallenged "self-identification" (Passel and Berman 1986). Discounting the "wannabes," the actual population of Indians living on reservations, and thus potential beneficiaries of self-government, was less than a quarter of the total, approximately 332,257.[34]

Socialism

Secretary James G. Watt created a furor in Indian country with controversial remarks on January 19, 1983 (Cook 1996, 16). Watt appeared on a talk show, *Conservative Counterpoint*, and said,

> We have tremendous problems on the Indian reservations. I frequently talk about it by telling people if you want an example of the failures of socialism, don't go to Russia—come to America and go to the Indian reservations . . . every social problem is exaggerated because of socialistic government policies on the reservations. . . . Terrible socialism. We ought to give them freedom, we ought to give them liberty, we ought to give them their rights, but we treat them as incompetent wards. . . . In the Great Society, we came in with all these legal aides and all these programs and made federal funds available to fund Indian governments. So if you're the chief or the chairman, you're interested in keeping this group of people assembled on a desert environment where there are no jobs, no agriculture potential, no water, because if the Indian were allowed to be liberated, they'd go and get a job and that guy wouldn't have his government handout as a government Indian paid official. They've become ward bosses.[35]

Watt's views of Indian government officials are in direct contradiction to the whole self-determination policy effort to develop effective tribal government. They are also reminiscent of earlier times in Indian policy. William Jones, Indian commissioner in 1900, had similarly said of Indian officials that he did not "want them to believe that the government would always serve as an employer of last resort, so he encouraged the replacement of agency Indian employees by whites" (Hagan 1997, 87). Turn-of-the-last-century commissioners Thomas Morgan and Francis Leupp had also "urged the Indians to leave the reservations, go where the work was, and not expect it to come to them" (Novack 1990, 648).

Although the Reagan administration was hostile to affirmative action in its civil rights policies, it did not thankfully go so far as to endorse this remarkable Indian "unpreference" policy implied by Watt (Detlefsen 1991; Shull 1993). Despite Watt's rhetoric, Indian preference continued to be pursued in federal hiring by the administration; in fact, by 1990, 83 percent of BIA employees were Indians, up from 78 percent in 1980 (Novack 1990, 653). There are those who have agreed with Watt that this is not necessarily a good thing. Economic historian Steven Novack suggests of the preference policy, "By an odd twist, the BIA had become a self-perpetuating bureaucracy, at least in part because preferential hiring had made it essential to the Indians" (1990, 650).

Not surprisingly, Indian leaders were instantly outraged over Watt's rough-hewn remarks. LaDonna Harris immediately wrote to the president, "He has undoubtedly undermined the spirit and intent of your policy, but even more damaging than that is the perpetuation of racist, stereotypical attitudes from the one man in the Federal government most intimately involved with American Indian people."[36] The next day on *Good Morning America,* several Indian spokespersons accused him of racism and called for his resignation. Watt defended his comments on that show and did not retract them.[37]

Watt made an impromptu address to the NCAI executive board on January 25, 1983, but here as in other forums, while he tried to put a good face on it, he did not explicitly retract the socialist and ward boss themes: "But I don't apologize for the message because the Indian people of America have been abused by the United States government for too many years, and we've got to bring about change." In fact, he himself felt abused: "And while I spoke out, I've been given abuse by the press. Terribly abused by the press. . . . I've taken the abuse of the press and some of your people who attacked my motives, my thoughts, my deeds, and my actions."[38]

He remained unrepentant; even after his resignation, he repeated the remark about socialism on the reservations in his retrospective book: "The sad truth of that statement has never been challenged. That I dared to tell the truth was what upset the liberals" (Watt 1985, 73). Watt left the administration in October 1983, but not because of his offensive remarks to such a small constituency as the American Indians. He had managed to offend almost everyone else as well, as for example in his comment on the diverse composition of an Interior Department commission, "I have a black, I have a woman, two Jews and a cripple" (Cannon 1991, 428).

Six days after Watt's Indian debacle, the presidential policy statement was released, on January 24, 1983, some suggest as an antidote to the bad press Watt generated (Cook 1996, 16). Although the statement had been prepared long before, the timing of the release does appear to be linked to Watt's remarks. Elizabeth Dole, then assistant to the president for the Office of Public Liaison, wrote the day after Watt's interview,

> The subject outcry by the media is highly exaggerated and contrived. The number of tribal leaders who have spoken out in opposition represent a small segment of the overall Indian community. . . . Admittedly, this does little to ease the pain of having to hear that the administration is anti-Indian and racist. Our Indian policy and its attendant statement are excellent, and we need not apologize nor be defensive. . . . The sooner we can release our statement the better, in order to enable our supporters to provide a counterpoint to criticism from a primarily radical fringe.[39]

It was released within four days.

The Presidential Message

The message begins by endorsing self-determination, as a form of New Federalism: "The administration believes that responsibilities and resources should be restored to the governments which are closest to the people served. This philosophy applies not only to State and local governments but also to Federally recognized American Indian tribes." It traces its lineage to the 1970 Nixon message and the 1975 act but suggests that little progress has been made in the eight years since 1975.[40]

The staff who prepared the message faithfully reflected Reagan's "bedrock convictions," including the notion that government is the problem rather than the solution. "Federal policies have by and large inhibited the political and economic development of the tribes. Excessive regulation and self-perpetuating bureaucracy have stifled local decision making, thwarted Indian control of Indian resources and promoted dependency rather than self-government. This administration intends to reverse this trend by removing the obstacles to self-government and by creating a more favorable environment for the development of healthy reservation economies." It also offers reassurance for those who fear termination. "Our policy is to reaffirm dealing with Indian tribes on a government to government basis and to pursue the policy of self-government for Indian tribes without threatening termination."[41]

The tribes are to receive more self-government but also must move toward more self-sufficiency. "It is important to the concept of self-government that tribes reduce their dependence on federal funds by providing a greater percentage of the cost of their self-government. . . . This administration pledges to assist tribes in strengthening their governments by removing the Federal impediments to tribal self-government and tribal resource development. Necessary Federal funds will continue to be available." As a concrete measure toward strengthening "those small tribes which have the greatest need to develop core governmental capacities," the message offers "the Small Tribes Initiative. This program will provide the financial support necessary to allow these tribes to develop basic tribal administrative and management capabilities."[42]

There were a number of specifics as well as the more general statements. In keeping with New Federalism, the administration pursued block grants to the states, some of which tribes were already eligible to apply for, but the message extends this. "The administration now proposes that Indian tribes be eligible for direct funding in the Title XX social services block, the block with the largest appropriation and the greatest flexibility in service delivery." Symbolically strengthening the government-to-government theme, "We are moving the White House liaison for federally recognized tribes from the Office of Public Liaison to the Office of Intergovernmental Affairs, which maintains liaison with State and local governments." Also symbolically important: "This administration calls upon Congress to replace House Concurrent Resolution 108 of the 83rd Congress, the resolution which established the now discredited policy of termination."[43]

Self-government is to be pursued but essential to this is economic development. "Indian leaders have told this administration that the development of reservation economies is their number one priority." This too is hindered by excessive federal regulation: "Developing reservation economies offers a special challenge; devising investment procedures consistent with the trust status, removing legal barriers which restrict the types of contracts tribes can enter into, and reducing the numerous and complex regulations which hinder economic growth." Ultimately, it is up to the tribes to pursue self-development as a form of self-determination: "Tribal governments have the responsibility to determine the extent and the methods of developing the tribe's natural resources." But in keeping with Reagan's more general economic ideas, "It is the free market which will supply the bulk of the capital investments required to develop tribal energy and other resources."[44]

In order to help the tribes in the task of development, "This administration . . . is establishing a Presidential Advisory Commission on Indian Reservation Economies. The Commission, composed of Tribal and private sector leaders, is to identify obstacles to economic growth in the public and private sector at all levels."[45] In fact this commission had already been announced some ten days before, a fact apparently overlooked in the haste to issue the presidential message.[46] Also, to help make all of this more efficient, "this administration directs the Cabinet Council on Human Resources to act as a mechanism to ensure that Federal activities are nonduplicative, cost effective, and consistent with the goal of encouraging self-government with a minimum of Federal interference."[47]

The message ends by making plain that the Indian policy program is simply part of the general Reagan policy for the nation as a whole. "This nation's economic health—and that of the tribes—depends on adopting this administration's full economic recovery program. This program calls for eliminating excessive federal spending and taxes, removing burdensome regulations, and establishing a sound monetary policy. A full economic recovery will unleash the potential strength of the private sector and ensure a vigorous economic climate for development which will benefit not only Indian people but all other Americans as well."[48] Indian policy is once again to serve as a microcosmic demonstration of larger scale presidential policy.

The initial reception in Indian country was mixed and to some extent overshadowed by the outrage over Secretary Watt. Officer suggests the Indian reception was "lukewarm" and comments, "Overall it was a conservative policy message with some positive features and no particularly negative ones, but Indians felt it left much unsaid" (1984, 98). Vine Deloria Jr. more harshly observed, "Reagan's gospel of reliance on the private sector is absurd when applied to reservations. . . . With the budget cutbacks it is not possible to have anything except instant misery on the reservations" (Deloria and Lytle 1984, 259). A group of congressmen, led by Morris Udall, sent a letter requesting a meeting: "We are deeply concerned that this Policy statement is far from adequate and offers little hope to the 1.4 million American Indians and Alaskan Natives of this nation."[49]

The Commission on Indian Reservation Economies

The presidential order creating the Commission on Indian Reservation Economies specified, "The Commission shall advise the President on what actions should be taken to develop a stronger private sector on Federally recognized Indian reservations, lessen tribal dependence on Federal monies and programs and reduce the Federal presence in Indian affairs." The charge goes on to indicate that "new Federal financial assistance" is not to be considered. The five items to be looked at:

> (1) Defining the existing Federal legislative, regulatory, and procedural obstacles to the creation of positive economic environments on Indian reservations. (2) Identifying and recommending changes or other remedial actions necessary to remove these obstacles. (3) Defining the obstacles at the State, local and tribal government levels which impede both Indian and non-Indian private sector investments on reservations. (4) Identifying actions which these levels of government could take to rectify the identified problems. (5) Recommending ways for the private sector, both Indian and non-Indian, to participate in the development and growth of reservation economies, including capital formation."[50]

Once again the problem is clearly too much government, and the solution is less of it. More spending is ruled out a priori.

Originally intended to complete its report by September 1983, the commission's efforts were extended and the report not actually delivered until November 1984.[51] Six of the nine members were of Indian ancestry, including the co-chair, Ross O. Swimmer, principal chief of the Cherokee. The other co-chair was Robert Robertson, who had headed the National Council on Indian Opportunity in the Nixon administration.[52] In contrast to the Abourezk AIPRC report's 206 recommendations, this report made only thirty-seven, all focused on the economic issue. The administration, however, seems not to have paid much further attention to these ideas after receiving the report (Cook 1996, 18).

True to its charter, the commission focused the report on obstacles to economic development and how they may be overcome. A pie chart allocates percentages of each obstacle: 32.9 percent due to the BIA, 21.7 percent due to other federal agencies, and 34.8 percent due to tribal government itself.[53] Tribal obstacles included

> Weak Business Management by Tribal Governments . . . Rapid turnover of Tribal Governments and Unfavorable Business Climate . . . Unskilled and Unreliable Indian Labor Force . . . Inadequate Infrastructure, Physical Resources, and Locational Incentives . . . Tribal Political Discrimination . . . Cultural Dissonance . . . Tribal Zoning and Environmental Enforcement . . . Tribal Sovereign Immunity to Suit . . . Indian Preference in Employment . . . Fractionated Heirship Land.[54]

Among the recommendations made to address these problems of tribal government were

> That tribal governments undertake a process of modernizing their constitutions to achieve an effective separation of powers in which the tribal judicial system can operate without political interference from tribal government; and in which there is an effective separation between the tribal executive and legislative branches of government. . . . That tribal governments undertake a process of separating their economic business functions from political or management interference by tribal governments.[55]

The commission also recommends "that Indian tribal governments make private ownership or private management of tribal enterprises an objective of their involvement in business activity."[56]

There are similar recommendations to reform the federal end of the federal-Indian relation to remove the obstacles to development found there. In sum, the commission suggests, "The changes anticipated by the recommendations made in this section contemplate a new Federal-Indian relationship, no longer characterized by paternalism, but imbued with a sense of partnership between the United States and Indian Tribal governments."[57] For those who fear that this new relationship might amount to termination, the report specifically calls for repeal of the termination resolution and recommends "that in the spirit of Indian self-determination which seeks to strengthen tribal autonomy and accountability and simultaneously protect tribal resources against termination. . . . Legislation [should create] an Indian trust services administration whose function is protection of Indian resources rather than management of Indian resources."[58]

Dawes Redo?

Despite many reassurances to the contrary, some still suspected that all this talk about less federal or even tribal government and more privatization would lead to termination, "termination by accountants," as C. Patrick Morris called it (1988).[59] But termination, when all is said and done, was almost entirely about saving money. The Reagan approach was much more ideological; in the manner of the artistic minimalist Bauhaus, less was thought to be more (Burt 1982; Fixico 1986). The appropriate historical comparison is perhaps to another era, that of the Christian Reformers of the nineteenth century, who gave us the 1887 Dawes Act, not simply to save federal money but for the good of the Indian people—less common land was more (Prucha 1976). Some have suggested that Reagan's general economic themes attempted to emulate and revive the frontier economy of the 1800s with its "bonanza economics" (Slotkin 1992, 646).

The key similarities between the nineteenth-century assimilationist views and the Reagan doctrines are in the emphasis on self-sufficiency, individualism at the expense of the collective, and a stress on private economic enterprise rather than communal. The commission report, sounding a tad Marxist, suggests, "Private ownership of tribal enterprises contemplates ownership of the means of production, private management, for profit motivation and freedom for individual Indians."[60] This can be compared to the policy enunciated by Interior Secretary Carl Schurz in 1879 "to foster the pride of individual ownership of property instead of their former dependence on the tribe, with its territory held in common" (Prucha 1984, 194). Compare also the statement of Henry Dawes about the Indians' lack of private property, "There is no selfishness, which is at the bottom of civilization," to the observation of financier Ivan Boeske (who many saw as an icon of the Reagan era), "Greed is healthy" (Washburn 1975, 17; Cannon 1991, 832).

"Reaganomics," as many called it, like the Dawes policy stressed the positive benefits of individual exploitation of Indian common lands.[61] This too was a reflection of larger Reagan policy favoring increased privatization and exploitation by entrepreneurs of all public lands, not just those held by Indians. Reagan noted of public lands in general, "We will move systematically to reduce the vast holdings of surplus land and real property since some of this property is not in use and would be of greater value if transferred to the private sector" (Hanke and Dowdle 1987, 114; Short 1989). The "tragedy of the commons" was something to be eliminated wherever it might be found, including on the reservations. The less ideological terminationists of the fifties were more willing to tolerate the collective, so long as it cost the government nothing, as witness cooperative mechanisms of Indian ownership like Menominee Enterprises Incorporated, formed in that era (Peroff 1982).

Land

The Dawes Act ultimately had the effect of stripping away some 90 million acres of land and crippling the American Indian resource base permanently (Washburn 1975). Despite the Reagan rhetoric, no similar large-scale land loss ever occurred in his administration; no significant amount of public lands or Indian resources were privatized. The administration did support a bill, the Ancient Indian Land Claims Settlement Act, which was designed to avoid emerging litigation over eastern lands. This was similar to the terminationist Indian Claims Act in that both substituted money for land. "The bill essentially extinguishes all ancient land rights and creates a mechanism for determining money payments."[62]

But the bill was opposed in Indian country and not passed by Congress. Although little actual land was lost, no significant lands were restored, unlike during the Nixon era, which saw significant restoration of sites like Taos Pueblo's Blue Lake (Gordon-McCutchan 1995).

Water

There were other assaults on common resources, as in the administration efforts to support the quantification of Indian water rights, a process started under Carter (McCool 1994, 238). One student notes, "Beset by a wavering court on one side and a deadlocked Congress on the other, nearly everyone now seems to be either guardedly or enthusiastically urging negotiation as the preferred method of settling Indian water rights—everyone, that is, except the Indians" (Burton 1991, 59). Another student has commented that Reagan's water policy "was consistent . . . with Ronald Reagan's sustained efforts to privatize reservation development" (McGuire 1992, 240). Like the Carter administration, the Reagan administration pursued a policy of negotiation but in fact achieved few settlements (McCool 2002, 47).

One successful negotiation, the Southern Arizona Water Rights Settlement Act, was vetoed by Reagan (McCool 1994, 235). He said on that occasion, "I strongly believe that the most appropriate means of resolving Indian water rights disputes is through negotiated settlement and legislation if it is needed to implement any such settlement. However, H.R. 5118 is a negotiated settlement with a serious flaw. The United States Government was never a party to the negotiations that led to the development of this proposal. . . . I pledge the full cooperation of my Administration to the States and local governments that are facing the difficult task of equitably resolving Indian water rights suits. I cannot, however, pledge the Federal Treasury as a panacea for this problem."[63] McCool notes, "The veto gave the President an opportunity to express his disapproval of the cost of the bill and to push for a rewrite that would shift some of the costs of the bill from federal to state and local sources" (1994, 236).

One of the comparatively few settlements actually reached was a modification of the 1978 settlement the Carter administration had reached with the Ak Chin. Reagan observed, "The Ak Chin settlement embodies three policies of this administration: first, that Indian tribal governments can and should decide what is best for their peoples; second that the complex issue of Indian water rights is better handled through negotiation than litigation; third, that we will fulfill our commitments in a fiscally responsible fashion." Language in the signing statement also clearly reflects the intent to free up surplus water for non-Indian users, as the Dawes Act sought to free up surplus land. The bill "provides that water not needed to satisfy the Ak-Chin entitlement will be available for allocation to other water users in central Arizona."[64]

Recognition

Some Indian groups continued to seek and receive recognition through the Federal Acknowledgment Process established during the Carter administration, the Narragansett of Rhode Island among them in 1983 (Prucha 2000, 304). Others, however, still sought legislative remedies, and one of these bills, recognizing the Mashantucket Pequot, was vetoed by Reagan. His principle objection seemed to be, as with the Southern Arizona water settlement, that the federal costs were too large and should be shifted to the state. "The claim that would be settled by this bill is not against the Federal Government but against the State of Connecticut, which sold the Indian land. . . . However the costs of the settlement proposed in this bill would be borne almost entirely by the Federal Government." He also questioned the tribe's recognition: "The Tribe may not meet the standard requirements for Federal recognition or services that are required of other tribes."[65]

As with the Southern Arizona settlement, the various parties to the Connecticut settlement hastily rewrote the bill to secure its veto-free passage. "Under the agreement, the state would put up more money, and the tribe would submit a petition, which would be given the most perfunctory review and [be] approved" (Campisi 1990, 185). The bill, the Connecticut Indian Claims Settlement Act, was signed by Reagan on October 18, 1983 (Benedict 2000, 144). As with Yaqui recognition in the Carter administration, the Federal Acknowledgement Process had been largely circumvented. Although the BIA had acquiesced, Jeff Benedict quotes a representative as commenting, "The department does not believe it can support any future legislation which would legislatively recognize a group of Indian descendents as a tribe unless it has had an adequate opportunity to review the historical and factual basis for the group's claim to tribal status" (2000, 144).

The Gay Head Wampanoag of Massachusetts were, for many of the same reasons, similarly denied an initial settlement in 1982. They and their congressional sponsors also rewrote it, and it was signed by Reagan August 21, 1987 (Campisi 1990, 192). The staff statement urging his approval of the revised bill noted, "Since then . . . (1) the group has received Federal acknowledgment as an Indian tribe; (2) the bill has been revised to require the state to contribute a 50 percent share of the settlement cost; (3) the Tribe's claim has been deemed of sufficient merit to be entertained by the courts; and (4) based on available data, the settlement sum appears to approximate the value of the Tribe's claim."[66]

As some tribes sought recognition, other tribes that had their federal status terminated in the fifties and sixties began to seek restoration of that status as the climate changed in Indian affairs. The best documented case and an inspiration to other tribes to make the attempt was that of the Menominee of Wisconsin, who were restored in 1974 (Peroff 1982; Castile 1998b, 148). The Klamath of Oregon began the process of pursuing restoration, with advice from some Menominee, in 1975 (Haynal 2000, 296). Courts had held that the terminated tribes retained their treaty rights, and the Klamath reformed their tribal government to administer these at that time. As with Menominee restoration and Yaqui recognition, the support of home-state representatives was critical in framing and pushing legislation. Interior and White House staff had no objections to the congressional bill, and August 27, 1986, the Klamath restoration bill was passed and signed into law by President Reagan.[67]

Indian Schools and Lands

Boarding schools had been being phased out in Indian education since the time of John Collier, and in the Reagan years, still more were spun off; from seventy-seven in 1928, there were only three federal boarding schools by the end of the Reagan era (Szasz 1999, 31, 216; Achuleta, Child, and Lomawaima 2000, 19). This led not so parenthetically to some loss of land formerly dedicated to Indian uses. The Phoenix Indian School, for example, held a large tract of valuable urban land, and the Reagan administration proposed closing it in its very first budget (Parker 1996; Trennert 1988). After some delay, it was closed, and there was something for everyone in the deal. The City of Phoenix got some of the Indian land as a park; the VA hospital got some land to expand, and the panther's share was opened to private development by the Barron-Collier Company (Parker 1996, 63–65).

I say panther's share rather than the cliched lion's share because the Barron-Collier Company got its piece of the Phoenix Indian land by trading lands they already held to the Park Service. They traded land in Florida, which they could not develop, which then became the Florida Panther Wildlife Refuge. The Indians did not make out as well as the panthers and alligators—their only direct benefit from the loss of land was a trust fund of $35 million dedicated to educating Arizona Indian children in public schools, arguably already a federal obligation under Collier-era Johnson O'Malley legislation (Parker 1996, 63–65).

Not only did the administration close boarding schools, but it transferred day schools to the states. In a 1983 listing of Indian Affairs accomplishments, "Transferred 17 Bureau of Indian Affairs day schools to the State of Alaska, achieving a savings to the Federal government of $5.9 million."[68] The Reagan administration sought in many areas to shift costs from the federal government to state and local government. By the end of the eighties, 90-plus percent of Indian students were attending non-federal public schools, a trend that had also been going on since the Collier era (Szasz 1999, 214; Prucha 2000, 315). Many have taken note of the cuts in federal spending for Indian education in the Reagan years, but that does not necessarily translate directly into lost education for Indian students because the states inevitably took up some of the slack (C. Morris 1988, 733; Cook 1996, 15).[69]

Although the Reagan administration didn't ultimately change much in Indian affairs, other than spending, it seemed to have put a damper on new federal Indian initiatives from other sources. Beginning in 1975, with the Self-Determination Act, the period until 1980 was one of considerable legislative and judicial activity in Indian affairs, most of them positive for American Indians (Prucha 2000). In the first Reagan term, the administration itself introduced very few bills, and Congress seems to have lost interest.

Casinos and Investigations
The Second Reagan Administration

*W*illiam P. Clark served as secretary of Interior for the remainder of Reagan's first term after Watt's resignation. In President Reagan's second term of office, he appointed Donald P. Hodel, former secretary of energy, as secretary of Interior. Pemberton notes, "Clark and Hodel were more politically sensitive than Watt, but they did not break sharply with his policies" (1997, 122). Ross O. Swimmer, who had been co-chair of the presidential Commission on Indian Reservation Economics, became the assistant secretary for Indian affairs in the second term and was also clearly committed to the general Reagan economic policies of reduced government and more free enterprise on the reservations, as outlined by that commission.[1]

Congressional resistance to administration proposals for cutting funding, including Indian program funding, tended to moderate their impact in both terms (Cook 1996, 16). In Reagan's first term, Republicans controlled the Senate but not the House, while in his second term, Democrats controlled both houses (Pemberton 1997, 146). Democrat Mo Udall was the chair of the House Interior and Insular Affairs Committee, responsible for Indian affairs, throughout both Reagan terms (Carson and Johnson 2001, 203). The Senate Select Committee on Indian Affairs was chaired by Republican William S. Cohen of Maine from 1981 to 1983, and Republican Mark Andrews of North Dakota took over from 1983 until 1987. Democrat Daniel K. Inouye of Hawaii became the chair in 1987, near the end of the Reagan era, and held it until 1995 (Wilkins 1995, 31). The rate at which Reagan introduced legislative change was lessened in his second term, and Congress was not particularly active, nothing like the Abourezk years, in either term.

More reports continued to appear. An Interior in-house task force on

Indian economic development, which began work in October 1984, de-livered its report in the second term, July 1986.[2] The primary charge was to follow up with recommendations to implement the presidential task force findings. This group was composed of personnel from Interior's Office of the Assistant Secretary for Policy, Budget, and Administration and various BIA policy staff.[3] Most of the report deals with pump-prim-ing activities such as the creation of enterprise zones, tax incentives, and the like. It also suggests the importance of "regulatory relief," saying "In-dian bingo, for example, reflects a special form of regulatory relief—an exemption from some of the normal state regulations controlling gam-bling."[4] Indian gaming was increasingly favorably viewed in the Reagan administration as an economic stimulus.

In addition to a wide range of specifics directly focused on economic development, the report made some general observations. Among these, the task force notes, "The most important long run actions that the Fed-eral government can take to promote Indian economic development may well involve improvement in Indian education," a view at some odds with the Reagan administration attempts to shift education out of the federal realm of responsibility. Sounding more Reaganesque, it also notes, "Be-yond education the most critical initiatives must come from Indian tribes and from individual Indian entrepreneurs."[5] Few of the recommenda-tions of this report or the earlier presidential commission were ever im-plemented. Of such studies, Donald D. Stull has commented, "The major reason for their limited impact is their inability to implement their rec-ommendations. Task force recommendations are implemented, if at all, piecemeal and in a watered-down condition" (1990, 208).

A Blueprint

The man principally in charge of such implementation in the second Reagan term was Ross Swimmer. Swimmer's views, visible in his activities as assistant secretary, are more cohesively expressed in an article he pre-pared in the last year of the administration, "A Blueprint for Economic Development in Indian Country" (1989). He notes pessimistically, "As the 'Reagan Revolution' began, it promised tax cuts, a smaller federal govern-ment, and more autonomy for local governments. . . . While the rest of the country responded to the tax cuts with renewed vigor, such responses did not occur as readily in Indian country. Business as usual, meaning tribal proposals for more money from Washington, continued to be the way of life on many reservations" (Ibid., 14). He notes that spending on Indian programs had actually increased since 1979, from 2.5 billion to 2.7.[6] "Yet services to Indians proportionally decreased because of the large increase in the number of tribal governments and eligible Indian population. . . . My own tribe, the Cherokee Nation of Oklahoma, grew in numbers from 20,483 in 1975 to 92,071 in 1987. . . . Why would someone identify himself as Indian today and not ten years ago? Obviously, there are many reasons, but certainly one major reason is the large increase in federal expenditures for Indians during the past twenty years" (Ibid., 15).

This increased expenditure, and Indians rallying to take advantage of it, is more problem than benefit in his and Reagan's model. "Indeed, checks from Washington often lead to a dependent relationship that is very difficult to sever. In fact, economic development is the antithesis of the kind of development that occurs when a federal bureaucracy gets into the act" (Swimmer 1989, 15). What is the real answer? "The first step in building a reservation economy is to give Indian tribes more control over their resources and charge them with the responsibility and accountability of putting these resources to good use. . . . In 1988 a proposal was made to Congress to modify the existing trust relationship to permit tribes to have an active management role with respect to their trust assets and for the BIA to assume a more passive role" (Ibid., 18).[7] Congress did not act on this suggestion.

He also identifies himself directly with one of the major programs of the termination era.

> The second step in building a reservation economy is to develop human resources. . . . The most effective program for finding work for Indian people in this century was known as the Relocation program. . . . This program encouraged people living on reservations to relocate to job markets, usually found in larger cities. . . . Today, however, we find many people returning to the reservations, not because tribal governments have created growing economies, but because the federal government has committed itself to the goal of providing food,

shelter, and health and welfare care to Indians that live there. This
policy, in turn, has led to a devastating state of dependency burden-
ing local economic development efforts. (Swimmer 1989, 19–20)

This is not only nostalgia for termination but remarkably reminiscent of Watt's comments about tribal leaders conspiring to keep their
constituents in the jobless desert. The solution to reservation economic
development, it seems, lies in its population leaving to find work elsewhere.

"The third step toward economic freedom for tribes is the responsible use of capital formation by tribal governments . . . $1.8 billion is on
deposit in the United States treasury. . . . This is an extraordinary amount
of money of which a fraction could fuel virtually any local economic
activity in this country" (Swimmer 1989, 20). This is in some contradiction to the view above that residents should seek work elsewhere and
also raises the question as to why Indian trust money will work more effectively than federal funds, which have previously failed in this task. The
bigger problem in his view is not the lack of capital, whatever its source,
but the use of it by the tribes. He suggests the presidential commission
found "the lack of understanding by tribal leadership about business in
general as the number one factor in retarding economic growth on Indian reservations" (Ibid., 21).

He goes on to point out the failures of the federal government in
addition to this critique of tribal government. True to the Reagan perspective, all government is problem and the market is solution. "Under
our economic system, government does not create wealth but rather uses
the wealth that has been created by others to provide necessary services
demanded by its citizens. Business does create wealth and must continue
to grow and expand in order to continue to create wealth for the government to tax" (Swimmer 1989, 26). He concludes the paper, "It is inexcus-
able that the first Americans should be at the bottom of the social, economic, and educational scale of our society. Indian people are entitled to
economic freedom as much as anyone else in this country" (Ibid., 31).

In addition to such economic development schemes, Swimmer continued to pursue the policy of withdrawing federal control over Indian

schools. In 1987 he put forward proposals that would have gradually turned over all Indian schools in several states either to the states or to Indian tribes themselves through contracts (Szasz 1999, 214). This proposal aroused strong opposition in Indian country, which led to congressional opposition and the withdrawal of the plan (Cook 1996, 20). Nonetheless, as noted in a *BIA Report on Indian Education* issued in 1988, increasingly the federal role in Indian education was primarily one of funding state and Indian contract schools rather than directly operating them (Prucha 2000, 316). The Reagan administration simply pushed a little harder in that long-standing direction than Congress and Indian country found comfortable.

The Senate Special Committee on Investigations

Yet another report on Indian affairs appeared in the second Reagan term, this one nongovernmental. Phoenix newspaper the *Arizona Republic* published an exposé series titled "Fraud in Indian Country: A Billion Dollar Betrayal" (Trahant, Hall, and Schaffer 1987). The indictment of the BIA was sweeping, to say the least. The paper's initial summary of the eight-day series captures its tone: "Today's installment explains how badly managed federal programs burden taxpayers and fail to serve Indians. Subsequent stories detail incompetence, deceit and corruption in federal Indian programs for education, health, housing, crime and economic development" (Ibid., October 4, A-1). The article's approach was scattered and often anecdotal, but the point was clear: The BIA was doing a bad job, and Indian reservations were in bad shape.

The newspaper series might have been just an eight-day wonder, but it led to yet another report.

Prompted by these and other reports of fraud and corruption, Chairman Daniel K. Inouye and his colleagues on the United States Senate Select Committee on Indian Affairs decided to investigate fraud, corruption and mismanagement in American Indian affairs, no matter where or to whom it led. Chairman Inouye, who combined a long standing commitment to Native American rights with extensive involvement in Senate investigation, moved quickly to establish a Special Committee on Investigations to uncover and root out these pernicious barriers to Indian self-determination.[8]

Inouye had just become chair after the Democrats regained control of the Senate. He appointed a bipartisan Committee on Investigations consisting of two Arizona Senators, Dennis DeConcini (Democrat) and John McCain (Republican), chair and co-chair, respectively. Thomas Daschle (Democrat) of South Dakota was the third member.

After some two years of investigations, the committee issued its report November 6, 1989, during the Bush administration. It called for a "New Federalism for American Indians," interesting terminology coming from a committee under Democratic control, since "New Federalism" was a domestic policy label largely preempted by Nixon and Reagan (Conlan 1988). The committee had investigated and reported on six areas of supposed mismanagement and fraud—Indian preference contracting, child abuse in schools, oil and other resource management, Indian health services, Indian housing, and tribal government itself. It offered a range of legislative recommendations in all these areas, and as with most such Indian reports, few of these were ever implemented.

Since most of the problems were attributed to failures of the existing federal system, particularly the BIA, the most sweeping solution suggested was to turn everything over to the tribes instead. They proposed setting up an Office of Federal-Tribal Relations within the executive office of the president, which would negotiate treatylike agreements—"the agreements will allow any tribe that so chooses to exit the current bureaucracy of Federal Indian programs and, instead, receive and use at its own discretion a proportional share of the current Federal Indian budget."[9] This is simply a more sweeping version of the self-determination block grants proposed by the Reagan administration in 1981, earlier by Senator Abourezk in 1978, and still earlier by Nixon in 1971. If fully implemented, however, it would have eliminated the BIA and other federal Indian offices entirely, arguably moving toward termination.

One of the problem areas addressed in the report was the past failures of the tribal governments themselves, now expected to take over all federal functions. Therefore, as part of the process of turning federal funds over to the tribes, there were recommendations to make them more accountable to both their members and the federal government. These included the requirement that "under the new agreements the American Indian tribes will agree to. . . . Operate their governments in accordance with written constitutions that adhere to the Indian Civil Rights Act and have been approved by a majority of all enrolled adult tribal members in a special ratification referendum; and . . . Publically report certified financial statements analyzing the budgets of their governments and all tribally owned businesses."[10] They also proposed new federal laws, including "to specifically proscribe the misappropriation of . . . federal funds by tribal governmental officials and employees as well as other misconduct by tribal officials and employees."[11] None of this occurred.

Tammany Indians?

Whether the Reagan administration's and congressional critiques of Indian governments were justified or not, there were problems with the new systems of self-government. Indian self-government had theoretically existed on most reservations since the Indian Reorganization Act of 1934, but as we have seen, until the seventies and the creation of the self-determination policy, these governments governed very little, all substantive decisions still being made by the bureau. In the seventies, these pro forma governments found themselves with real control over substantial resources and jobs though the contracting process. With something worth fighting over, Indian leaders and their followers did indeed engage in intensified factional fighting (Castile 1998b, 131). The ensuing political scramble among factions and individuals "to get something for the people" has been described to some extent by Bee and by Fowler (Bee 1979, 1990; Fowler 1982, 2002).

Paradoxically the success of the self-determination policy in strengthening tribal governments had also created a whole new range of problems for those governments and their leaders, as Vine Deloria Jr. notes: "During the sixties the War on Poverty brought many new patronage jobs to the reservations and the tribal chairman's position became even more critical in reservation politics . . . so the fight for tribal chairman became nearly an armed conflict between opposing groups of Sioux" (1974,

70). Bee notes of the Quechuan frequent demands for recall elections: "The typical grounds for a recall attempt were alleged acts of personal misconduct, which could cover anything from allegations of misappropriation to failure to approve a personal loan" (1990, 57). Fowler notes of the Cheyenne Arapaho, "Here as in other Native American communities, both tribal and federal courts and the Department of Interior have been flooded with petitions to overturn elections, remove or prosecute tribal officials, overturn decisions made by tribal officials, and so on" (2002, xiv).

The internal struggles generated by the new empowerment can perhaps be compared to the early days of ethnic politics in the United States, in the mid-1800s, when the leaders of new immigrant groups, like the Irish, first achieved political leverage and clout. New structures of self-government in new hands, in both immigrant and Indian cases, suffered growing pains, as the new systems took some time to perfect and the neophyte politicians were not always paragons of civic virtue (Allen 1993, 27). Judging by the rhetoric of tribal politics, at times in the seventies and eighties, the reservations seemed to be generating their own versions of New York's Tammany Hall, with its bosses, cronyism, and corruption (Allen 1993).[12] One example is the case of Navajo Peter MacDonald, considered in the Senate report.

The Rise and Fall of MacDonald

Despite Watt's and Swimmer's objection to the creation of federally funded jobs on the reservation by the Great Society programs, most in Indian country tended to view this as a positive phenomenon. Many skilled and well-educated American Indians were able to find professional-level work at home rather than being forced to wander afield. Among the new leaders drawn back into reservation life was the Navajo Peter MacDonald, lured from work as an engineer in California to a role in the Navajo Office of Economic Opportunity (MacDonald 1993, 154). From his role as head of that office, he became chair of the tribe. "He served three four-year terms until 1983, throughout the era when tribal governments were transformed into modern full fledged governments supported by extensive federal funds. . . . He helped usher in the new era of tribal government to the Navajo people."[13] He also, unfortunately, in the view of Senate investigators, became something of an exemplar of the failures of Indian self-government.

MacDonald, a Republican, was seriously considered for commissioner of Indian affairs by the Nixon administration (Castile 1998b, 88). He was also at least initially in favor with the Reagan administration, which among other things formally recognized the World War II role of Navajo code talkers, for which MacDonald had trained, and sent him a certificate of recognition on their behalf.[14] A Reagan aide wrote of him in 1982, "Peter MacDonald has been most cooperative and helpful. He supported Reagan in 1980 and organized Indian support for the Watt nomination."[15]

MacDonald, however, was very much out of favor with Republican Senator Barry Goldwater of Arizona. Goldwater suggested to White House staff that "Chairman Peter MacDonald of the Navajo Nation will undoubtedly approach you in an effort to offset the ruling made against him on the Navajo-Hopi land dispute. . . . So don't give him an inch." Goldwater also wrote to presidential aide Elizabeth Dole to say, "Peter MacDonald is personally obnoxious to me. . . . I do not like the White House putting him in any position for which he could gain advantages to help him in his re-election."[16]

There is little question that during MacDonald's initial two terms as Navajo chair, the power and influence of that office much increased, in large part because of contracting under the self-determination policy. "We were ultimately able to control far more of the services affecting our people. During Raymond Nakai's last year in office, when BIA service contract arrangements did not exist, his budget had included $30 million in tribal funds and $100,000 in government funds. By 1976, the annual tribal budget was over $60 million, and we had over $100 million in funds from the profitable government contracts" (MacDonald 1993, 221). His success, however, seems to have turned MacDonald's head, as evident in his own characterization of his first two terms.

As chairman of the Navajo Nation I had all the power that accompanies the ruler of a country. People sought political favors from me. People were anxious to do my bidding. I could get someone out of

jail or influence a governor to release someone from a state peniten-
tiary. I had access to the president, to senators and representatives. I
could travel internationally and be received by heads of state. I was
in charge of a police force. I was the executive who oversaw a budget
of millions and millions of dollars. I had access to perquisites that
made my daily life easy while others struggled in hardship. . . . I, as
chairman, had literally moved mountains, fed the poor, built houses,
provided water, and established scholarships for previously unedu-
cated youths. (MacDonald 1993, 239)

Heady stuff, and apparently, according to Senate investigators,
enough to lead him into abuse of these new self-determination-era
powers.

After a term out of office, MacDonald was elected once more to a
fourth term of the chairmanship in 1986, but he soon found himself actively under scrutiny by the Senate Special Committee on Investigations.
With the increased responsibility of the tribal governments had come
increased possibilities of corruption. MacDonald noted of the Navajo, "it
is only in the last forty years that the number of employees and their responsibilities have grown to the level where it is possible to bribe people"
(1993, 258). He also suggested that the Navajo had no traditions governing bribery. "The Navajo consider gifts as expressions of love and respect,
nothing more. There were no tribal laws governing the giving of gifts"
(1993, 258). The Senate investigators noted, "As with any other recently
emerging government or indeed country, newly found power affords opportunity for its abuse. At the same time, checks and balances to thwart
individual corrupt officials have not had the same opportunity to develop."[17] The prime, indeed almost the only, example of corrupt officials
examined by the committee was MacDonald.

Although other matters in his administration were questioned, the
purchase by the Navajo tribe of Big Boquillas Ranch was the ultimate
source of MacDonald's downfall. Admitting that third parties profited by
purchasing the land and then reselling it at an inflated price to the tribe,
MacDonald insisted that this was necessary because "the only way we
could get adequate credit to buy Big Bo in 1987 was through third party
involvement. . . . Brown and Tracy made almost $8 million in windfall

profit by flipping the land sale. And the Navajo Nation obtained land that would otherwise been impossible to get" (1993, 278–79). As to the charges that he benefited from loans and gifts from the third parties? "Did I benefit as a result of the two men's actions? There is no question they were trying to influence my decision. Ultimately I acted in the manner I thought best, even though that meant paying an inflated price for the land" (1993, 279).

The Senate investigation, however, gathered evidence through tape recordings and immunized testimony of participants suggesting MacDonald had been soliciting bribes. "The tape recordings of these meetings confirmed that the Big Bo sale was viewed by MacDonald as simply a way to enrich himself."[18] In the end the Senate investigators concluded that MacDonald had been guilty of "massive wrongdoing."[19] The committee turned its material over to the Justice Department, and eventually MacDonald was convicted in both federal and tribal courts, on racketeering and contributing to riots at Window Rock in the federal courts, and accepting bribes in the tribal court (*Time* 1993, 11; Iverson 2002, Ch. 8; Wilkins 2003, 215–16).[20] Although the investigation led to the personal downfall of one tribal chair, MacDonald, the committee's more sweeping ideas for reform of tribal government were never enacted.

Courts and Casinos

The conflict between the states and the Indian tribes embedded within their boundaries has been extensively explored by Biolsi, for the Rosebud Sioux, in a book titled *Deadliest Enemies* (2001). Biolsi takes his title from the 1886 Supreme Court case *United States v. Kagama,* in which the Court noted of the tribes, "They owe no allegiance to the States and receive from them no protection. Because of the local ill feeling, the people of the states where they are found are often their deadliest enemies" (Prucha 2000, 167). Federalism, whether new or old, in Indian country is ultimately about a three-handed relationship—federal-state-tribal (McCulloch 1994). A dramatic illustration of the tension with the states is the struggle over Indian gaming.

The Seminole had raised questions in the courts as to the limits of state authority over Indian gaming in 1978, at the end of the Carter administration. Other tribes also began to operate bingo halls and also faced challenges in the courts from state authorities seeking to prohibit or regulate them (Mason 2000, 47), all of which reached a head in the conflict between the state of California and some of its tribes, including the Cabazon and Morongo bands, which began in 1980 and reached the Supreme Court by 1987 (Ibid., 49). In *California v. the Cabazon Band of Mission Indians,* the Supreme Court finally held for the Indians' right to operate their gaming enterprises free of state regulation (Getches, Wilkinson, and Williams 1998, 742).

California was among those states who had criminal jurisdiction over Indian reservations granted by the termination-era Public Law 280, in 1953 (Prucha 2000, 234). The courts, beginning with the Seminole case, had wrestled with the issue of whether this applied to gaming. In the Seminole case in 1980, "the district court held that Florida's gaming laws were civil/regulatory, not criminal/prohibitory. Therefore, notwithstanding the state's assumption of criminal jurisdiction over Indians on Florida reservations under P.L. 93-280, the state limits on bingo did not apply to the Seminole games" (Mason 2000, 47). In *Cabazon,* the Supreme Court came to much the same conclusion: "If the intent of a state law is generally to prohibit certain conduct, it falls within P.L. 280's grant of criminal jurisdiction, but if the state law generally permits the conduct at issue, subject to regulation, it must be classified as civil/regulatory and P.L. 280 does not authorize its enforcement on an Indian reservation. The shorthand test is whether the conduct at issue violates the State's public policy" (Getches, Wilkinson, and Williams 1998, 744).

As the states were contending with the tribes in the courts over gaming regulation, the federal government in the form of the Reagan administration was far more supportive of Indian gaming. Very much concerned with new forms of economic enterprise on the reservations, there was a tendency to see gaming positively, as a new revenue resource (Wilkins 2002, 116; Cooper 1996, 614). By 1986 the Interior in-house task force was considering the possible benefits of Indian bingo.[21] Mason notes, "To the extent that the Reagan administration had a position on Indian gaming, it involved regulatory concerns balancing state, federal, and Indian interests, promotion of Indian gaming as part of its overall policy emphasizing economic development, and the elimination or reduction of possible criminal activity" (2000, 59). Although there was some ambivalent rhetoric, de facto the Reagan administration supported the development of Indian gaming.

The Supreme Court itself noted this federal support in *Cabazon,* citing "the congressional goal of Indian self-government, including its 'overriding goal' of encouraging tribal self-sufficiency and economic development. These are important federal interests. They were reaffirmed by the President's 1983 Statement on Indian policy. More specifically, the Department of Interior, which has the primary responsibility for carrying out the Federal Government's trust obligations to Indian tribes, has sought to implement these policies by promoting tribal bingo enterprises" (Getches, Wilkinson, and Williams 1998, 746).

The court noted specifics, including a consistent pattern by the BIA and other federal agencies of approving grants and loans for the operation of bingo facilities, and the approval by the BIA of tribal ordinances and contracts related to these (Getches, Wilkinson, and Williams 1998, 746). However, the administration did lean toward limiting Indian gaming solely to bingo.[22] "The decision that California could not regulate reservation gaming meant essentially that no state could, because no state had more authority to regulate reservation activities than P.L. 280 states" (Pevar 2002, 320). The *Cabazon* decision effectively left reservation gaming free of external controls because the only possible restraints were federal, and there were no such regulations in place.

Congress had first begun to consider bills regulating Indian gaming in 1983, when Mo Udall introduced a bill (Mason 2000, 54). Other bills were considered, but it was not until after *Cabazon* that serious and hurried efforts were made to limit the Indian's newly won freedom. Nevada Senator Harry Reid, a major player in creating the legislation, noted, "Following the Supreme Court's ruling in the *Cabazon* case though, there was little choice except for Congress to enact laws regulating gaming on Indian lands. The alternative would have been for the rapid and uncontrolled expansion of unregulated casino type gambling on Indian lands" (Reid 1990, 17).

Although the eventual bill was complex and dealt with a variety of issues, the critical one was the role of the states versus the role of the tribes, as Reid illustrates:

I began discussions with Chairman Daniel Inouye (D-Hawaii) and Chairman Morris Udall (D-Arizona), the Senate Indian Affairs Committee and the House Interior Committee chairs respectively. . . . State and local government officials and law officers felt that they had to have some role in saying that Indian gaming did not have detrimental effects on their citizens. To deal with this problem I suggested to Chairman Inouye that we use the concept of Tribal-State compacts. . . . Under such compacts, states and tribes, as if they were foreign entities, would negotiate the regulatory structure for Class III gaming. (Reid 1990, 18–19)

The final bill, a compromise between tribal sovereignty and that of the states, did include the compacting requirement. The bill created three classes of gaming and a National Indian Gaming Commission to oversee the regulation of some of these. Class one comprised traditional Indian social games that would be regulated only by the tribes; class two included games like bingo that would be regulated by the tribes and the new commission; class three, essentially casino gambling, was subject to compacts negotiated with the states (Mason 2000, 65). The purposes of the act were set out in three parts, capturing most of the issues debated:

(1) to provide a statutory basis for the operation of gaming by Indian tribes as a means of promoting economic development, self-sufficiency, and strong tribal governments;

(2) to provide a statutory basis for the regulation of gaming by an Indian tribe adequate to shield it from organized crime and other corrupting influences, to ensure that the Indian tribe is the primary beneficiary of the gaming operation, and to assure that gaming is conducted fairly and honestly by both the operator and the players; and

(3) to declare that the establishment of independent Federal regulatory authority for gaming on Indians lands, the establishment of Federal standards for gaming on Indian lands, and the establishment of a National Indian Gaming Commission are necessary to meet congressional concerns regarding gaming and to protect such gaming as a means of generating tribal revenue. (Prucha 2000, 323)

There was considerable opposition to the bill among Indians who felt it unfairly limited the sovereignty that had been affirmed by *Cabazon* (Levin 1997). For example, Wendell Chino, then chair of the Mescalero Apache, wrote Reagan to urge his veto: "The Indian gaming bill, S.555, claims to take away our Indian Tribal governments' power to regulate our own gaming activities. It forces State and Federal government regulatory jurisdiction on us . . . we believe it is unconstitutional. It desecrates fundamental principles of Indian self-determination and Tribal sovereignty law."[23]

The administration was ambivalent. "As the Departments of the Interior and Justice advise, S. 555 is the product of years of negotiation between the tribes, the States and the concerned Federal agencies. Although both departments have expressed concerns about the enrolled bill, they have concluded that this legislation represents the best that can be expected of the affected parties and Congress."[24] Although the administration was generally opposed to federal regulation of anything, the bill did promote tribal economic self-sufficiency, a major administration goal, so Reagan signed the Indian Gaming Regulatory Act (IGRA) into law October 17, 1988 (Prucha 2000, 322).[25]

The main virtue of Indian gaming was obviously the increased revenue to the impoverished tribes, but probably no one anticipated at the time the enormous growth in the size of the revenues at stake. "From 1988 when IGRA was passed, to 1997, tribal gambling revenues grew more than 30-fold, from $212 million to $6.7 billion"[26]—an undoubted economic success, but one that continued to be shrouded in controversy. Many were opposed not simply to Indian gaming but to gaming itself. I. Nelson Rose notes of the debate over IGRA, "The problem was not that it was Indian gambling, but that it was gambling, period" (1990, 5). Indians themselves were also ambivalent about gambling, and some tribes have refused to enter into the enterprise, most notably the Navajo (Anders 1998, 104; Goodman 1995, 119).[27]

American Indians in precontact times undoubtedly engaged in a variety of gambling games; however, these games were not the basis of the new tribal enterprises (Gabriel 1996). The core repertoire, in addition to bingo, depends on Vegas casino-style card games and slots. These are far from traditional; indeed, card playing was one of the items introduced by Evil One that the Iroquois prophet Handsome Lake warned against: "These cards will make them gamble away their wealth and idle their time" (Pasquaretta 2003, 128). In fact, some studies have suggested a rise in compulsive gambling behavior among reservation peoples (Cozzetto and Larocque 1996). In the same cautionary spirit, American Indian author Gerald Vizenor has observed, "The casinos have raised new contradictions, the envy of outsiders, and the bereavement of traditional tribal values" (Vizenor 1992, 412).

Just as the new powers of tribal governments under self-determination created new conflicts, these new gambling resources have had similar effects. "Internal conflicts generated by gaming have become bitter and divisive—and sometimes violent. Accusations have been flying on some reservations that tribal officials have stolen funds from the casino, or have refused to allow certain families to enroll their children . . . in order to increase the size of their own per capita payments" (Pevar 2002, 328). Still, after the failure of nearly two generations of economic development efforts on the reservations, many tribal leaders were ready to try almost anything, from toxic and radioactive waste storage to gambling, regardless of opposition (Brosnan 1996, Hanson 2001).

Despite the problems many still feel, "Gaming offers . . . the most likely source of sustained economic successes for impoverished tribes" (Jorgensen 1998, 169). Although recognizing the unsavory aspects of gambling (calling it gaming does not help), some Indian leaders and supporters, like Senator James Abourezk, have taken a damn-the-torpedoes view: "If individuals like Donald Trump and the variety of other private casino owners are allowed to pocket gambling money, then by God so should the Indian tribes if they choose to do so" (Lane 1995, xix). An aide claimed that Mo Udall felt similarly: "The Indian Gaming Act most certainly caused a moral dilemma for Udall. He opposed government-backed gambling. Still, he believed in Indian sovereignty, and felt if the states could do it, the tribes should have the same right" (Carson and Johnson 2001, 205).

Even as an economic resource, the casinos have problems, largely in the unevenness of benefit distribution. Those Indian casinos near large population centers prosper; those off the beaten track generally do not (Goldin 1999, 851). Unfortunately, given the U.S. history of removal and

relocation, the largest tribes, with the greatest poverty, are located on isolated lands in the West. For such western tribes, casino revenues are comparatively small, and their generally larger tribal population makes the
per capita impact also comparatively small. As a result, those who need
it most are the least likely to benefit, since the new buffalo does not graze
on their lands, which raises policy questions of how to focus or redistrib-
ute the impact of gambling revenues.

The major impact of the new gambling revenues tends to be concentrated in the hands of a few of the smaller tribes conveniently located
near cities. Twenty years after the start of the Indian gaming boom, according to the data collected by the National Gambling Impact Study
(NGIS), 188 tribes had gambling of some sort, while 368 had none at
all. The total take was $6.68 billion in 1997, but twenty of the well-situ-
ated tribes got 50 percent of that. While the amount taken in is roughly
equivalent to all federal spending on Indian programs, unlike those programs, it is not distributed evenly in Indian country, whether measured
by tribe or per capita. The Pequot, for example, got about $1 billion of
the $6.68—for the benefit of some 529 members (Spilde 1999, 11).[28] The
debate over gaming goes on.[29]

In addition to *Cabazon,* the Supreme Court delivered one other major decision of significance in Indian affairs during the Reagan administration, *Lyng v. Northwest Indian Cemetery Protective Association,* in April
1988 (Prucha 2000, 318). The First Amendment of the Constitution states,
"Congress shall make no law respecting an establishment of religion or
prohibiting the free exercise thereof" (Pevar 2002, 261). Several California
Indian groups brought suit under the free exercise clause to prevent the
construction of a logging road through areas of national forest they held
to be sacred. They also appealed to the American Indian Religious Freedom Act (AIRFA) of 1978 as an additional basis to protect these sacred
sites.

The Supreme Court in *Lyng* disagreed that either the Constitution or
the AIRFA prevented the road: "The Constitution simply does not provide a principle that could justify upholding respondent's legal claims. .
. . Whatever rights the Indians may have to the use of the area, however,
those rights do not divest the Government of its right to use what is,
after all, its land" (Getches, Wilkinson, and Williams 1998, 758–59). As to

the AIRFA, the Court recognized its injunction to government agencies to be "solicitous" of Indian religion and said, "It is hard to see how the Government could have been more solicitous," but "Nowhere in the law is there so much as a hint of any intent to create a course of action or any judicially enforceable individual rights" (Getches, Wilkinson, and Williams 1998, 760). Indian groups immediately began to lobby Congress to overturn *Lyng* with legislation amending the AIRFA, with no success in the Reagan administration.

Congressional Revival

In the last year of the Reagan presidency, Congress seems to have begun to revive from its legislative lethargy in Indian matters.[30] The Alaska Native Claims Settlement Act was amended to extend protections and native choices in 1988 (Prucha 2000, 314). Like the twenty-year trust restrictions of the Dawes Act, resource protections under the Alaska Native Claims Settlement Act of 1971 were due to expire in 1991. Many feared a replay of the Dawes era, stripping away unprotected Indian lands and resources, so the amendments allowed the native groups themselves to determine when and how restrictions on stock and land should be eased (Getches, Wilkinson, and Williams 1998, 910).

The Tribally Controlled Schools Act, also in 1988, following the theme of increasing self-determination, widened the ability of tribes to administer school contracts (Prucha 2000, 320). It also parenthetically at long last formally repudiated HCR 108, the "termination resolution," which had been a Reagan pledge. In Section 5203, "Declaration of Policy," part (f) "Termination," the act declares that "The Congress hereby repudiates and rejects House Concurrent Resolution 108 of the 83rd Congress and any policy of unilateral termination of Federal relations with any Indian Nation" (Prucha 2000, 321). Like the termination resolution itself, this resolution had no force as law; plenary authority remained, but it was a reassuring gesture.

In response to Indian complaints about the difficulties of contracting procedures, Mo Udall sponsored a bill in 1987 to amend the 1975 Self-Determination Act. In the hearings, native leaders' comments were nearly universally approving of the self-determination concept and nearly universally condemning of its implementation by the BIA. The focus of the amendments and the hearings was procedural rather than conceptual—the main topic was the problem of the provision of "indirect costs" to the tribes (Dean and Webster 2000).[31] The staff memo to Reagan recommends his approval of the bill and notes, "Many tribes believe . . . the Act subjects them to excessively burdensome administrative requirements related to contracting, and fails to insure they receive adequate funding to pay indirect contracting costs . . . H.R. 1233 would amend the act to remove many requirements that are objectionable to the tribes."[32]

Negotiations between Interior, Congress, and several tribes led to including in the amendments of the Self-Determination Act Title II—"Tribal Self-Governance Demonstration Project" (Prucha 2000, 322). This authorized the secretary of the interior to negotiate with up to twenty tribes to enter on an experimental basis into five-year contracts wherein the tribes could administer any and all federal programs as they chose. In fact this created the block grants of the Nixon-Abourezk-Reagan proposals of years before, but only for a few tribes. It in no way guaranteed these in perpetuity or abrogated existing trust responsibilities, nor did it significantly reduce the federal bureaucratic establishment.

Interior was largely supportive and had worked with Congress to create the demonstration bill. The Justice Department, however, had some difficulties with some of the specifications and requirements laid upon the executive branch and recommended language to be added to the signing statement.[33] Reagan did approve the bill, and his signing statement did incorporate the Justice objections to the congressional requirements on the executive branch, saying, for example, of one of them, "this unconstitutional provision is severable from and does not affect the otherwise constitutional provisions of this act."[34] Self-determination was still the policy of both president and Congress, and in this bill, both worked to make it a reality.

In 1984 Reagan had vetoed amendments to the Indian Health Care Act of 1976.[35] Congress in 1988 once again proposed similar amendments. Reagan commented, "Four years ago, I vetoed the Indian Health Care Amendments of 1984 because it contained a number of seriously objectionable provisions. Unfortunately, H.R. 5261 not only includes most of these provisions but also adds new objectionable ones."[36] Among other

things, he objected to special provisions for Hawaiians as racial preferences. He had similar objections to Congress's proposed Indian Housing
Act of 1988 but did sign that bill. There the objection was "that 'Indian
families' are singled out for special assistance as members of a racial
group, rather than as members of quasi-sovereign entities."[37]

Join Us?

In keeping with his image as the Teflon president, Reagan encountered
remarkably little fallout from his distinctly odd remarks about Indian
affairs in Moscow in May 1988. In June, asked a question about them, he
said, "I don't know just what the specific complaint is, but I know that
we have been doing for a long time our utmost to provide education for
those who wanted to maintain Indian life on the reservation, in contrast
to those who leave and come out and join the rest of us and become
more like us."[38] Aides also attempted to explain his Moscow remarks:
"The President was making a point about the rights of American Indians
to be free and not be forced to assimilate into the non-Indian culture. He
was also educating an audience about the human rights and the freedoms
all American enjoy."[39] Ross Swimmer suggested, "The President should
be judged by the record of service his administration has rendered to the
American Indian people."[40]

Even as local tribal governments gained increased authority under
the self-determination policy, national-level Indian leadership seems to
have fallen into some disarray in the Reagan years. Some national leaders
such as Vine Deloria Jr. and LaDonna Harris, who were very influential in
the Nixon years, were apparently little heeded by the Reagan administration. The NTCA, as noted above, lost its federal funding and ceased to exist. The NCAI, however, remained the principal Indian lobbyist voice and
was joined by the Native American Rights Fund (NARF). NARF was a
spinoff of OEO-sponsored legal-aid programs and pursued Indian interests in the courts rather than as lobbyists (Castile 1998b, 35; NARF 2005).

AIM, at the height of its media influence in the early seventies, had
by the Reagan years descended into near political irrelevance. It had never had much in the way of a coherent program, and by the eighties had
even less direction. AIM was reduced to media opportunism, only getting
brief attention when things Native American came into national focus.
For example, during the Reagan campaign against the Sandinista regime

in Nicaragua, AIM got involved, on both sides. Russell Means spoke out for the Miskito Indians associated with the Contras, while other AIM leaders spoke out for the Sandinista "Spanish" (Castile 1988; Means 1995, 463).

Despite odd remarks and struggles over schools and funding, even at the very end of his administration Reagan still seemed able to muster the support of some Indian leaders. Partly to make up for his gaffe in Moscow, Reagan's staff arranged a carefully orchestrated meeting for him with some American Indians. Representatives of the Hopi, Mississippi Choctaw, and Cherokee met with Reagan in December 1988, and all made more or less positive remarks. Wilma Mankiller, "principal chief of the Cherokee Nation, said the administration policy of self-determination works and should continue. 'We are looking for a Federal partnership, not handouts.'"[41]

A Kinder, Gentler Indian Policy?

The Bush Administration

*D*uring his presidential campaign, George Herbert Walker Bush's staff prepared a very general statement on Indian policy, which promised to improve education and economy for the reservations and endorsed self-government.[1] They also prepared a letter to be sent to Indian leaders, which cited and endorsed the Republican Party platform statement. "We support self-determination for Indian Tribes in managing their own affairs and resources. Recognizing the government-to-government trust responsibility, we will work to end dependency fostered by federal controls."[2] The letter also said, however, "I believe strongly in the continuance of the legacy of President Abraham Lincoln, who fully recognized the importance of Indian sovereignty in a nation of sovereign states."[3]

Lincoln is a very poor choice as champion of either Indian or state sovereignty. Prucha notes of Civil War–era Indian policy, "The Lincoln government met the challenges by continuing the fundamental policies of the preceding decades: an absolute commitment to the transformation of the Indians into the white man's civilization and the development of the restricted reservations as the principal 'first step' in that process" (1984, 412). He also notes, "Lincoln himself devoted little personal attention to Indian affairs . . . he held common white views about their destiny," which was of course assimilation (Ibid., 413). Lincoln's stand on the limited sovereignty of the states and the war to enforce it also surely offers no legacy to comfort supporters of Indian sovereignty.

George Bush had served as vice president through the two Reagan terms of office. In this capacity, he had no active role in Indian matters, nor had he when in Congress or in any of his other governmental positions (Parmet 2000). His autobiographical works do not mention Indian affairs nor do any of his major biographers (Bush 1987, 1999, 2001). As president he took no personal hand in Indian matters, nor was his administration particularly active in the area (Greene 2000). Bush was more concerned with foreign policy than with domestic policy in general and took little action in minority affairs, including Indian affairs. In the extreme view, "Some people said there was no domestic policy. Others called it moribund or, my favorite word, 'inert'" (Kolb 1994, 165).

Laffin characterizes the Bush administration as the "contractor presidency," which "describes situations where the president subcontracts policy and management to a cabinet secretary" (1996, 551). In effect, he suggests Bush was pursuing "cabinet government" as it was called in the Carter administration, at least in the case of some activist appointees. But in his study of three of these, "A fourth secretary with a non-activist reputation was also included as a contrast, Manuel Lujan. . . . Unlike the three others, he was appointed to maintain the policy status quo and dampen controversy" (Laffin 1996, 551–52). Lujan, as Interior secretary, had primary cabinet-level responsibility for Indian matters and in fact did not originate any significant new policies in Indian affairs.

Manuel Lujan chose Eddie F. Brown, a Pascua Yaqui, as assistant secretary for Indian affairs, and both served throughout Bush's term.[4] Cliff Alderman and Mary McClure, White House staff members with the Office of Intergovernmental Affairs, handled most of the Indian matters, among other things forming an interagency task force to coordinate policy.[5] As chapter 4 describes, members of the Special Committee on Investigations of the Select Committee on Indian Affairs wrote the White House to urge coordination of Indian policy through a White House staff arrangement, much like what already existed.[6]

They also enclosed a letter sent to their committee by President Richard Nixon, urging the formation of an independent Indian trust council authority to represent Indian interests, one of the proposals of his own administration that never materialized (see Castile 1998b, 94). Nixon noted, "Our goal in 1970 was to replace Federal programs that were ineffective and also demeaning to these Americans with policies that would give them more control over their own destinies. As President, I took special pride in supporting the policy of 'Self-Determination without Termination,' whereby my administration endorsed Indian control and responsibility over government service programs."[7] Nixon, as I have previously suggested, is the only modern president to take a personal interest in Indian affairs, which obviously he had continued doing in his post-presidency.

Indian leaders and members of Congress called on President Bush to issue a statement of his stand on Indian affairs.[8] In response to one of these, staff referred to the Reagan Indian policy statement, "President Bush, as a member of the Reagan administration, supported this policy and still supports it."[9] Earlier, in a letter to the NCAI, Bush said, "I . . . reaffirm my administration's strong commitment to Indian self-determination, and the government-to-government principles set forth by President Nixon in 1970 and expanded upon by President Reagan in 1983."[10] After a meeting with Indian leaders in April 1991, where they again requested a policy statement, the staff did issue an Indian message, on June 14, 1991 (FCNL 1991, 1).[11] The message was brief enough to cite in its entirety.

> On January 24, 1983, the Reagan-Bush administration issued a statement on Indian policy recognizing and reaffirming a government-to-government relationship between Indian tribes and the Federal Government. This relationship is the cornerstone of the Bush-Quayle administration's policy of fostering tribal self-government and self-determination.
>
> This government-to-government relationship is the result of sovereign and independent tribal governments being incorporated into the fabric of our nation, of Indian tribes becoming what our courts have come to refer to as quasi-sovereign domestic dependent nations. Over the years the relationship has flourished, grown, and evolved into a vibrant partnership in which over 500 tribal governments stand shoulder to shoulder with the other governmental units that form our Republic.
>
> This is now a relationship in which tribal governments may choose to assume the administration of numerous Federal programs pursuant to the 1975 Indian Self-Determination and Education Assistance Act.

This is a partnership in which an Office of Self-Governance has been established in the Department of the Interior and given the responsibility of working with tribes to craft creative ways of transferring decision-making powers over tribal government functions from the Department to tribal governments.

An Office of American Indian Trust will be established in the Department of the Interior and given the responsibility of overseeing the trust responsibility of the Department and of insuring that no Departmental action will be taken that will adversely affect or destroy those physical assets that the Federal Government holds in trust for the tribes.

I take pride in acknowledging and reaffirming the existence and durability of our unique government-to-government relationship.

Within the White House I have designated a senior staff member, my Director of Intergovernmental Affairs, as my personal liaison with all Indian tribes. While it is not possible for a president or his small staff to deal directly with the multiplicity of issues and problems presented by each of the 510 tribal entities in the Nation now recognized by and dealing with the Department of the Interior, the White House will continue to interact with Indian tribes on an intergovernmental basis.

The concepts of forced termination and excessive dependency on the Federal Government must now be relegated, once and for all, to the history books. Today we move forward toward a permanent relationship of understanding and trust, a relationship in which the tribes of the Nation sit in positions of dependent sovereignty along with the other governments that compose the family that is America.[12]

Some have characterized Bush's policies as simply continuing those of the Reagan era, as the "guardianship" presidency or "status quo" presidency (Duffy and Goodgame 1992; Mervin 1996). This is obviously partly true in Indian affairs inasmuch as his earlier staff statements and his presidential message consistently identifies with the Reagan policies. However, the strong Reagan emphasis on economic development leading to self-sufficiency with consequent reduction in federal support is conspicuously absent. The stress is on Indian governmental self-determination as an end in itself, not as a step toward fiscal independence. There is a strong endorsement of the government-to-government concept and of Indian sovereignty, except for the use of the modifiers "quasi" and "dependent." The message was generally well received in Indian country, LaDonna Harris commenting, "The significance of this timely response is that it gives an appropriate administrative legitimacy to Tribal governments."[13]

Indian affairs may not have gotten a lot of attention in the Bush administration, but what they did get were an improvement on the Reagan era. Samuel R. Cook notes, "The Bush administration will not be remembered for strong Indian policy initiatives. However, it must be credited for reversing some of the pejorative trends of the Reagan administration in Indian affairs, such as the reduction of the federal Indian budget and the diminished emphasis on Indian education" (1996, 23). Similarly Margaret Connell Szasz notes, "The harshness of Reagan's Indian policy lost some of its sharp edges under George Bush's 'kinder more gentler nation.' The budget restrictions enforced under Reagan relaxed slightly. To Bush's credit, he also encouraged contracting between tribes and the federal government" (1999, 217).[14]

Bush had vowed in his campaign to seek a "kinder, gentler America" and to be the "education President" (Quirk 1991, 82). The first of these goals is difficult to measure, but his hopes for national educational change were largely unrealized. Very few of Bush's proposals for education or in other domestic policy areas managed to survive a hostile Democratic Congress (Mervin 1996, 205). Bush struggled with Congress through the use of the veto and curiously through the signing statement. "Rather than to exercise his constitutional power of objection, these statements declared about the newly enacted law that particular provisions had 'no binding force in law.'" (Tiefer 1994, 3). Several Indian bills have such signing statements, which declare certain aspects of them unconstitutional or otherwise null and void; there are only two pocket vetoes.[15]

Examples of fudged Indian signing statements include "I am very concerned, however, that section 2 (a) (6) of the bill authorizes racial preferences, divorced from any requirement of tribal membership, and that will not meet judicial scrutiny under the Constitution."[16] In another, "The Constitution grants to the President the power to recommend to the Congress such measures as he judges necessary and expedient. Because of this power, provisions such as the one contained in this bill have been treated as advisory and not mandatory. I will, therefore, interpret section 106 (b) accordingly."[17] In yet another, "I am concerned, however, about provisions in this bill that provide benefits to 'Native Hawaiians' as defined in a race-based fashion. This race-based classification cannot be supported as an exercise of the constitutional authority granted to the Congress to benefit Native Americans as members of tribes."[18]

Reagan too had objected to legislation he perceived as "race based." Inasmuch as Hawaii is a part of the United States, some argue that its native peoples are "native Americans," but the courts have held that they do not have the special relation with the federal government of the other native peoples (Getches, Wilkinson, and Williams 1998, 944). Most recently, the Supreme Court in *Rice v. Cayetano* held that the special status of Indians was political, while that of the Hawaiians was racial and thus violated the Fifteenth Amendment equal protection clause (Kapur 2004, 422). The native Hawaiians have continued to seek recognition as having the same status as Indians, without success at the time of this writing.[19]

Generally, the members of the Indian subcommittees have been western congressmen from states with significant Indian reservation populations. Senator Inouye, chair after 1987, is an exception since the state of Hawaii does not have reservation populations. Inouye was active on behalf of the natives of his state long before becoming a member of the Indian committee. Bee notes that in 1977, "Senator Inouye of Hawaii introduced four bills that year to extend certain Indian education, CETA, self-determination, and financing programs to Native Hawaiians" (Bee 1982, 111). After 1987, as chair, he continued to attempt to graft native Hawaiians onto legislation dealing with Indian matters.

Water

The policy of quantification, negotiation, and settlement of Indian water rights continued largely unchanged in the Bush administration. Early on in the signing statement for the settlement of Puyallup land claims, Bush said, "The administration expects to continue to work toward settlements of legitimate Indian land and water rights claims to which the Federal government is a party."[20] He praised the process of negotiation in signing the Fort Hall Water Rights Act of 1990: "I applaud the spirit of compromise that allowed the parties to resolve their differences without the need to resort to the costly and often divisive litigation by which many other western water disputes are resolved."[21]

The administration did try to formalize the largely ad hoc process and issued written guidelines as *Criteria and Procedures* in 1990. "They standardized an organizing and reporting procedure that streamlined negotiations and made the whole process more manageable and efficient" (McCool 2002, 120). Lack of funding for the settlements continued to be a problem. One issue that was debated during the administration was the question of the source of the settlement funds. In general, money awarded for water settlements came from other areas of Indian funding, a zero-sum process. McCool notes, "there is no net gain in Indian country as a result of the settlements; money has been diverted from Indian housing, Indian education, and other trust responsibilities to fund the water settlements. . . . Eddie Brown . . . called it 'a tax on other Indian programs'" (2002, 62). The problem was not resolved by further special funding in the Bush administration.

Education

As part of the administration's attempts to live up to the education presidency concept, the secretary of education, Lauro F. Cavasos, called for a task force in 1989, the Indian Nations at Risk Task Force, to look into Indian education (Reyner and Eder 2004, 311; Szasz 1999, 217). The group held extensive hearings and issued a report in 1991 that gave impetus to a national conference on Indian education.[22] Congress in 1988 had called for a White House conference on Indian education as part of a more sweeping education bill, and several congressmen wrote to urge the administration to hold the gathering.[23] "Caught in the complex communication network linking Indian country, Congress, the White House and the Departments of Education and Interior, the conference which emanated from congressional legislation (PL 100-297) passed on April 28, 1988, materialized on

January 22–24, 1992" (Szasz 1999, 219).[24] This gathering too issued a report.[25]

Szasz views this process positively: "Any student concerned with the status of American Indian and Alaska Native education in the 1990s must begin with the material compiled through the INAR Task Force . . . the delegates to the White House conference left their imprint on the future" (1999, 218, 223). Vine Deloria Jr. is more pessimistic about the impact of this and other such reports: "In authorizing the report the secretary of education is following an age-old and revered tradition in Indian education. It is better to talk about education than to educate. The ink will hardly be dry on this report before another organization, or another federal agency, has the urge to investigate, and the cycle will begin again" (2001, 151).

The authorizing legislation for the conference called on the White House to deliver a report and recommendations at its conclusion, which it did on October 9, 1992.[26] It said, among other things,

> the administration certainly finds more room for agreement with the Delegates than for disagreement. The President agrees, for example, that early childhood education, safe and drug-free schools, and reducing the number of school dropouts are all key ingredients to improving education in America. . . . While the administration cannot agree to recommend funding for all the requests for new money in the report, it strongly supports the call for reform and for shake-up of the status quo. In addition while some recommendations are supportable in principle, they must be addressed in the regular tribal, federal departmental and congressional budget formulation processes.[27]

The one definite outcome was the decision not to support a National Board of Indian Education, which the conference had been charged to consider (Szasz 1999, 223). The administration's general agreement in principle with the report, but without further funding and with an admonition to go through channels, did not lead to any sweeping changes in Indian education during the Bush administration. True to Deloria's predictions, a similar conference was held yet again in 1995 in the Clinton presidency to discuss the same reports and findings. At that conference,

Szasz notes of the delegates, "their frustration emerged in phrases such as, 'Here we go again' and 'Why are we doing this again?'" (1999, 226).

The Bush administration also approved the reauthorization of the Tribally Controlled Community College Assistance Act of 1978, but with some controversy. Sections 1102–05 of the bill encouraged the use of Native languages in schools and public proceedings. Senator Slade Gorton wrote urging its veto: "This bill encourages not just bilingualism but multilingualism, the abandonment of English and the further impoverishment of Native Americans at the hands of their own tribal bureaucracies."[28]

Bush did sign the bill but included some hedging language. "I also note that section 105 of the act provides that the right of Native Americans to express themselves through the use of Native American Languages shall not be restricted in any public proceeding. . . . I construe this provision as a statement of general policy and do not understand it to confer a private right of action on any individual or group."[29] A separate Native American Languages Act of 1992 was also later approved, with Bush saying, "Traditional languages are an important part of this Nation's culture and history and can help provide Native Americans with a sense of identity and pride in their heritage."[30]

BIA Reorganization

As discussed in the last chapter, the Special Committee on Investigations found massive failure of the BIA to serve Indians and noted "at least 42 congressional investigations have recommended federal reorganization, restructuring, retinkering. And in one nine year period alone, the BIA was actually reorganized ten times."[31] The committee proposed abolishing the bureau and other federal Indian bureaucracies entirely and turning the money over to the tribes as a permanent entitlement, but this radical step was never seriously considered, and instead, predictably enough, another round of discussion about reorganization of the BIA followed the report.

One major proposed change was to create a new layer of offices under the direction of the assistant secretary for Indian affairs, and in particular to create a more autonomous office of Indian education.[32] Lujan arranged a meeting of over eight hundred tribal leaders to discuss the proposals but was met with considerable hostility to the plan. One of the major complaints was lack of consultation, about which Philip S. Deloria noted, "The sense of being aggrieved is part of the relationship, and it manifests itself in complaints about consultation."[33] The complaint of lack of consultation on Indian education matters is clearly symbolic in view of the administration's ongoing task force efforts.

The basic and central policy of self-determination remained unaltered. Congress did pass the Tribal Self-Governance Demonstration Project Act, which Bush signed on December 4, 1991. This bill extended the term of the existing demonstrations from five years to eight, and authorized the increase of participating tribes from 20 to 30 (Johnson and Hamilton 1995).[34] Similarly, having amended the Alaska Native Claims Settlement Act of 1971 in 1988 to extend its protection, Congress in 1990 created an Alaska Native Commission to further examine the condition of these peoples (Prucha 2000, 329). This commission did not issue its report until 1994.

Congress, with both houses now firmly in the hands of the Democratic Party, continued the relatively high level of activity in Indian affairs started in the last days of the Reagan administration. Although there was considerable activity, it was mostly in the form of the continuation and elaboration of existing policy rather than fundamental new directions. There were, however, some interesting new initiatives.

The National Museum of the American Indian

The Museum of the American Indian–Heye Foundation was established in New York in 1916 by George G. Heye to house his own enormous collections. By 1977 the collections were in some disarray, and the trustees were looking for a new location for the museum, which led to a struggle with state and local politicians and the American Museum of Natural History (Force 1999). By 1986 Mo Udall had introduced a bill to provide a home for the museum in the New York custom house, and David Rockefeller solicited President Reagan's support for that location (Force 1999, 343, 364). Roland Force, the director of the museum in 1987, heard of Senator Daniel Inouye's interest in a suitable memorial for Indians on the mall and proposed establishing a museum there, which Inouye soon began to advocate (1999, 373).

Inouye, with the support of John McCain, introduced a bill into the Senate (S 1722) in 1987 to establish the museum (Force 1999, 401). Colorado representative Ben Nighthorse Campbell joined Mo Udall as co-sponsor of the House version and became very much involved in ne- gotiations with the Congressional Black Caucus to secure space on the mall they had considered for a slavery museum (Viola 2002, 258). Inouye said at the hearings, "There will be a great museum established on the National mall that will be home to the most priceless artifacts of Indian culture, history and art" (Force 1999, 402). New York sought to keep the Heye collections at home, and eventually a compromise was reached to relocate some of them to the customs house as well as establishing a new museum on the mall.

There was still further discussion with the Smithsonian over the affiliation with that institution, and provisions were built in to require the museum to inventory collections with an eye to repatriation, fore- shadowing the Native American Graves Protection and Repatriation Act (NAGPRA; Trope and Echo-Hawk 2001, 21). In the end the bill was passed as the National Museum of the American Indian Act (Prucha 2000, 325). President Bush signed it into law on November 28, 1989, saying, "From this point, our Nation will go forward with a new and richer understand- ing of the heritage, culture and values of the peoples of the Americas of Indian ancestry."[35] Although the impact of the museum on the Indian peoples was entirely symbolic, it was an important symbol indeed.[36]

The Native American Graves Protection and Repatriation Act

Indian activists in the seventies and eighties increasingly targeted archae- ology and archaeological museum collections over the issue of cultural property; to whom belong the remains of the past? (Ferguson 1996, 68; Thomas 2000, 210) Legislation to resolve the issue was first introduced in 1986, and archaeologists, museum administrators, and American Indians engaged in heated debate until passage of the act in 1990 (Sharamitaro 2001, 123; Trope and Echo-Hawk 2001, 20–21). Congress considered sev- eral variations of the bill, but in the end a compromise was worked out between Indian representatives such as Suzan Shown Harjo of NCAI and representatives of the American Association of Museums and the Society of American Archaeology, facilitated by Mo Udall (Sharamitaro 2001, 124; Carson and Johnson 2001, 206).

In 1990 Congress passed NAGPRA (Prucha 2000, 332). The bill expands on the requirements of the 1979 Archaeological Resources and Protection Act that American Indians be consulted before excavation on federal lands. "NAGPRA gives Native Americans property rights in grave goods and cultural patrimony, as well as the right to repatriate human remains from federal and Indian lands" (Ferguson 1996, 66). The act did not apply to private lands. The provisions of NAGPRA have continued to be debated in the field of archaeology if not by the general public (Bray 2001, Clark 1999, Ferguson 1996, Meighan 1994, Nafziger and Dobkins 1999, Thomas 2000).[37]

The Indian Arts and Crafts Act of 1990

As Indians became "groovy" in the sixties, interest in their arts and crafts surged, a demand satisfied in part by the importation of replicas sold as the real thing (Castile 1998b, 115; G. Sheffield 1997, 3). Congressional sentiment grew to protect the true Indian craftsperson from the false, which inevitably led to an attempt to specify "who is an Indian" for artistic purposes, much as the acknowledgment process had sought to determine "who is a tribe" for self-government purposes (Castile 1996). The Supreme Court in *Santa Clara Pueblo v. Martinez* had ruled that tribes have a right to determine their own membership, and in the end that principle was extended to the determination of who is a tribal artist as well (Pevar 2002, 92).

The bill to regulate the authenticity of Indian arts was sponsored by Representative Ben Campbell, himself an artist and enrolled member of the Northern Cheyenne Tribe (Viola 2002, 191). Similar to the NAGPRA extension of Indian control over cultural patrimony, the Indian Arts and Crafts Act (IACA) extends tribal control over certification of art attributed to tribal peoples. The bill created criminal penalties and gave teeth to the regulatory powers of the Indian Arts and Crafts Board, in being since the 1930s (Schrader 1983; Prucha 2000, 334). In the process, however, the bill raised questions regarding Indian identity and its regulation.[38]

There was considerable debate and contentious testimony from Indian artists of a wide range of tribal affiliations and the unaffiliated (G. Sheffield 1997). In the end, the debate was reflected in the language of the bill: "The term 'Indian' means any individual who is a member of an Indian tribe, or for the purposes of this section is certified as an Indian artisan by an Indian tribe" (Prucha 2000, 335). This certification process was added to accommodate unenrolled artists who were none-theless acceptable to the tribes. Also, "tribe" was not limited to federally recognized tribes but was extended to "any Indian group that has been formally recognized as an Indian tribe by a State legislature" (Ibid., 335), this last apparently at the behest of congressmen from eastern states with state-recognized tribes (G. Sheffield 1997, 63).

As a result of this act, Indians, or Indian artists at least, became the only card-carrying ethnic group in the United States, forced to present their "papers" to display their art publicly (Barker 2003; Castile 1996; Gar-routte 2003, 18). Sponsor Ben Campbell declared, "All in all . . . the bill has been acclaimed by the tribes and the vast majority of Indian artists. Only a few so called Cherokees who could not prove ancestry have claimed that it is unfair" (Viola 2002, 191). Subsequent to the act, favorable senti-ment among native peoples was not nearly as universal as Campbell sug-gests (Barker 2003, 26).

Ironically, Campbell's own tribal membership, only acquired in 1980, is apparently not based on the sort of documentary proof that the act requires. According to his biographer, Campbell was de facto adopted in midlife by a Cheyenne family called Black Horse, who then testified to their undocumented relationship to Campbell in order to gain his tribal enrollment in 1980 (Viola 2002, 130).[39] Campbell presented his memories of his father's tales of Indian ancestry to the Black Horse family and re-counted, "Alec thought my father's mother was his older half sister. Who the hell knows? All Indians attach great importance to the oral tradition and to the knowledge of the tribal historians and storytellers. I don't have any way of knowing the real story" (Viola 2002, 127). Herman J. Viola conducted archival research into Campbell's genealogy during the writing of his biography, saying, "the search for Ben Campbell's roots was, to put it modestly, an archival challenge"; in fact no documents were found to pin down his supposed Cheyenne connections, to "prove ancestry," as he would phrase it (2002, 104).

Viola did reconstruct a story of possible relationships, but "perhaps all this is only a remarkable coincidence, perhaps not, but proving any of it at this late date is probably impossible, because any potentially useful tribal records at Lame Deer burned in a fire in 1958" (2002, 128). Viola also conducted interviews at Lame Deer in 1991: "The trip shed little light on his genealogy, but it demonstrated how completely the Northern Cheyennes had accepted him" (2002, 131). In the end this acceptance seems to have been more important to Campbell and the Cheyenne than paper proofs. "As for Campbell, establishing a technically pristine paper trail was never a high priority. He believed he had found the right family back in the late sixties, and that was all that mattered to him and the Northern Cheyenne" (Viola 2002, 138). But as a result of the IACA legislation, sponsored by Campbell, such pristine paper trails now mattered a great deal for other Indian artists.

Good-Bye, Columbus

Campbell was also influential in another matter in the Bush years. The quincentenary, in 1992, of Columbus's arrival in the New World was accompanied by considerable public celebration. Some American Indians took exception to the events, finding little positive to celebrate in the voyage of Columbus (González 1992).[40] Suzan Harjo, in a *Newsweek* special issue largely dedicated to pro-Columbus sentiment, noted, "For Native people, this half millennium of land grabs and one-cent treaty sales has been no bargain" (Harjo 1991, 32). The 1992 Alliance, with Harjo as its national coordinator, attempted to lend some focus to the various counter-demonstrations to the Columbus festivities.[41]

One event that caused particular acrimony, and protest from native activists, was the invitation to Columbus descendant Cristobal Colon to act as grand marshal for the Pasadena Rose Parade (Viola 2002, 282). This situation was largely defused when the Rose Parade officials responded to the protest by inviting Ben Campbell to act as co–grand marshall (Ibid.,

288). Despite opposition from some native protestors, Campbell accepted and rode at the head of the parade in traditional Cheyenne dress. Viola notes of Campbell's participation, "For his part, Campbell felt strongly that Indians would gain nothing by boycotting, disrupting, or blocking the event. 'The buffalo are not coming back,' Campbell said. 'We need to participate and be able to tell our story, and that simply can't be done if we drop out of the system'" (Viola 2002, 288).

In 1991 President Bush had declared a National Indian Heritage Month, saying, "This month, we also celebrate the unique government-to-government relationship that exists between Indian tribes and the Federal government. . . . We will continue to seek greater mutual understanding and trust in this relationship, as well as the further advancement of tribal self-government."[42] In response to the debate over Columbus, Bush then declared 1992 the Year of the American Indian, saying, "This year gives us the opportunity to recognize the special place that Native Americans hold in our society, to affirm the right of Indian tribes to exist as sovereign entities, and to seek greater mutual understanding and trust. Therefore we gratefully salute all American Indians, expressing our support for tribal self-determination and assisting with efforts to celebrate and preserve each tribe's unique cultural heritage."[43]

Epilogue

*I*n 1968 LBJ declared the policy of self-determination, reannounced (rather than reaffirmed) by Nixon in 1970, and embedded in law in 1975 in the presidency of Gerald Ford. It has since been endorsed by every subsequent president.[1] The law was amended in 1988, in 1994, and again in 2000 in attempts to streamline the process, but the basics of the policy have remained much the same, and it remains in force to the present day. As of 2000, the Senate unanimously passed a resolution saying, "Indian self-determination policy has endured as the most successful policy of the United States in dealing with Indian tribes because it rejects the failed policies of termination and paternalism" and resolved "that the Senate of the United States recognized the unique role of the Indian tribes and their members in the United States, and commemorates the vision and leadership of President Nixon, and every succeeding President in fostering the policy of Indian Self-Determination."[2]

As I attempt to examine in this book, between 1975 and 1993, self-determination became entrenched as official federal policy. Both Democrats and Republicans claimed responsibility for its origins, and it enjoyed bipartisan support throughout this period.[3] Yet despite near universal political support, there remained problems with the self-determination policy. One of these problems was the practical matter of implementation, turning policy into reality on the reservations, which turned out to be surprisingly difficult. The other problem was more philosophical; there remained continuing confusion as to what self-determination might actually mean, to both tribes and federal government.

The Implementation of Self-Determination

Starting with the OEO contracts in the sixties, there was general enthusiasm from the beginning among American Indian leaders for the policy (Castile 1998b, 35, 41). Given this and a favorable national political climate, one might expect a rapid move to complete tribal self-administration after a short transitional period. But the actual progress toward self-administration often seemed to be limited and slow. By 1993, nearly twenty years after it became law in 1975, the tribes were still administering only about one third of the BIA and Indian Health Service (IHS) program budgets; two thirds of the contractable remained uncontracted.[4] Some few tribes, mainly those in the self-governance experimental group, were administering many of the programs available for their reservations, but by no means all. While there was a considerable range, many tribes were still administering very little.

Why such limited progress? Debates over the policy during the congressional hearings in 1988 and in 1994 focused largely on procedural and funding problems in implementing the policy. The lack of money, notably the debate about overhead funding, was seen as a primary issue (Dean and Webster 2000). Over this period of considerable policy change, there was in fact little change in overall federal spending for Indian affairs; indeed there was a slight decline as measured in constant dollars (CRS 1998, 271; Stuart 1990, 8). Both those who supported the policy because it might save federal funds and those who expected it to increase funds were disappointed.

The BIA was the usual suspect, accused of resisting implementation. Those who thought the bureau would quickly wither away after 1975 were certainly mistaken. In 1994, despite the 1988 attempts to streamline the self-administration process, Representative Bill Richardson commented, "Tribal attempts to assume the operation of Federal programs have been hindered by an increased Federal operation of Federal programs, and they have been hindered by an increased Federal bureaucracy as well as by restrictive and unnecessary contracting regulations."[5] Senator McCain, who introduced new streamlining legislation in 1994, was even blunter in his critique of the bureau: "I find the conduct of the BIA and the IHS under this administration and under previous administrations to be outrageous. . . . So I regret to tell you, Mr. Chairman, that instead of moving forward we seem to be moving backwards, as the imposition of more regulations has taken place."[6] The BIA defended itself, complaining among other things that Congress itself had complicated matters by calling for elaborate procedures of tribal consultation.[7]

At the time of McCain's remarks in 1994, the failure of the BIA to promulgate new regulations, called for six years earlier, in 1988, is certainly remarkable, but the bureau as villain is an oversimplification, as is the "few dollars more" approach. No doubt it is true that bureau procedures slowed things down, but probably no more than any other federal bureaucracy. Even if the bureau were to become a very model of simplicity and efficiency, dispensing much-increased funds, it is doubtful that would completely solve the implementation problem. Some of the difficulties obviously must lie with the tribal end of things, not just with the bureau or funding. It is likely, for example, that some applications for programs are held up not out of federal bureaucratic ineptitude, but simply because they are bad applications—incomplete, unrealistic, and so forth.

In fact, many tribes were not even submitting applications that asked for all or even most of the potential programs they could be entitled to self-administer. Why the reluctance? One reason is perhaps a lingering suspicion that too much success at self-determination could lead back to termination. Fixico, a leading scholar of the termination era, is among those who have equated the two policies: "Simply put, self-determination implies termination" (1986, 203). Similarly, Philip S. Deloria has commented of the self-determination era, "Anyone who wonders whether termination is still alive need only ask whether a separate Indian political and legal existence will be tolerated in this country if Indian people are no longer poor or viewed by the majority as being culturally distinct" (Philp 1986, 192).

In this fearful perspective, the end of paternalism and the end of dependency that self-determination policy makers speak of can be made to sound like the preconditions for abandonment of federal support for tribal existence. There are similarities, at least rhetorically, in the calls for Indian self-government in the termination and self-determination eras, and some people clearly suspect the motivation to be the same as well.

Biolsi, for example, suggests that the effect of increasing tribal responsibility is "the offloading of obligations for the welfare of Indian people
from the federal or state governments or the nation at large" (2004, 244).
There is little question that if tribes were entirely self-administered and
economically self-supporting, the political conditions for Congress to
end the special relationship would be more favorable than before.

The failure to apply for complete self-administration is also doubt-
lessly linked to the problem of tribal governmental capacity to manage
the programs. Tribes wisely do not apply for programs they cannot manage. Tribal governmental capabilities and institutions needed to plan for
federal grants and properly administer them did not exist before the programs of the OEO in the sixties. The process of developing them has ac-
celerated since the Self-Determination Act in 1975, but twenty years is not
a long time to develop traditions of responsible self-government and an
administrative and political class to carry them out. As Stephen Cornell
and Joseph P. Kalt note, "For sovereignty to have practical effects in Indian
country, tribes have to develop effective governing institutions of their
own" (1998, 5).

Some have even noted an increase in the instability of Indian governments in recent times, which may be related to the self-administration
process (Bee 1990; Fowler 2002). Paradoxically, the self-determination
policy may be both cause and cure for this state of tribal disarray. John
Collier optimistically noted, "The experience of responsible democracy
is, of all experiences, the most therapeutic, the most disciplinary, the
most dynamogenic and the most productive of efficiency" (Collier 1947,
262). In the short run however, self-determination may have introduced
increased instability, primarily through factional infighting over control
of the new programs. As the case of Peter MacDonald illustrates, the vastly increased control of resources, particularly jobs, by tribal chairs has led
to more to fight about.

Note too the increased conflict between newly empowered tribal
authority and the local non-Indian jurisdictions with which it interacts,
particularly the states (Ashley and Hubbard 2004). Imre Sutton suggests,
"It is clear that as self-determination prevails as a government-to-government relationship between tribes and all levels of government—federal,
state, and local—more problems over jurisdiction and sovereignty and

hence more litigation will occur" (Sutton 2001, 257). Ultimately, it makes sense for tribes to cooperate and work with all such levels of government, but just what the new relationships are to be remains in a state of flux, and working it out contributes to the slow pace of change.

A small experienced and trained administrative class appears to be developing on the reservations to cope with the new possibilities, but is it handicapped by political instability? There are very few studies of the impact of self-determination policy on tribal government, but in one of the few, Bee suggests that, for the Quechuan, the role of political instability is not as great as might be expected. Although council seats and the chairmanship turn over frequently between factions, "A wholesale spoils system has not developed that dumps planners and grants people along with defeated rivals. . . . Their contribution is too important and skilled replacements are hard to come by" (Bee 1990, 61; Fowler 2002, xiv). In fact, in many places since the sixties, a sort of de facto civil service has grown up, focused on the grant process, attracting home the skilled and educated from off-reservation jobs, as was the case with Peter MacDonald.

In the context of the federal recognition debate, Ada Deer observed, "My opinion is, a tribe is a tribe is a tribe" (Castile 2002, 414). Similarly, many policy makers seem to feel that all tribes are alike in the self-determination process. Yet let us recall that one of the criticisms of the 1934 Indian Reorganization Act was its attempts to impose nearly identical constitutions on all tribes. Although the self-determination legislation by contrast allows tribes to adopt self-administration, in amounts of their choosing and at their own pace, I suspect in the minds of many in both tribes and Congress, there remains the expectation that they will all eventually end in the same place—complete self-governance.

However, it may simply not be true, for self-administration purposes, that a tribe is a tribe is a tribe, and perhaps one size does not fit all, and not all tribes can or will end up with identical and equally complete self-government. Indeed, that seems obvious on the face of it: A system of governmental institutions that might be workable for the Navajo, with their contiguous state-size territory and large resident population of hundreds of thousands, will certainly not be identical to that of a California tribelet with a dispersed population of a hundred and a reservation of a few acres. Ross Swimmer noted of such a small tribe that it had "no potential to be a self-sustaining economy . . . the tribe shares the economy with the surrounding county and nearby city" (1989, 16).

So too such small groups probably must share their administration with their neighbors. They have no realistic need for, nor the capacity to administer, the complete apparatus of self-sustaining governance—their own courts, police, fire department, and so forth. They would more logically share many of these functions with other nearby tribes and with other levels of nontribal government. That is the way things are done under BIA administration of clusters of small tribes and probably could best be done under tribal auspices. The extent of the interdependence will vary depending on size and other factors. The complexity of working out just how much self-government is enough and for whom is doubtless also one of the elements slowing the transition envisioned by the self-determination legislation.

The Meaning of Self-Determination

Part of the problem of implementation might lie in more profound disagreement on what it is that needs to be implemented. It seems fairly clear from the wording of the legislation and the various presidential policy statements that to the federal government, self-determination means self-administration. The tribes are to take over existing federally funded programs on their reservations as contractors in the manner of the OEO community action agency procedures that spawned the policy in the first place. Republicans tended to talk of this in terms of New Federalism and block grants, but it is the same idea as the OEO—Indians administering federal programs in their own communities with federal money.

This is not exactly self-determination, if by that you mean complete autonomy of local groups in making decisions about their own governance, because the tribes remain dependent on federal funds. Most reservations have underdeveloped economies that cannot generate tax revenues to support local services in the way other local governments are able to do. On most larger rural reservations, government—federal and tribal—is the major employer, not tax-paying private enterprises.[8] The programs for which federal funds are available and the amount of funding appropriated for them remains completely outside tribal control. They can apply for and administer only what Congress has approved and appropriated, and while there is a degree of consultation with Indian leaders, it is not Indians but Congress who makes these decisions.

The McCain-DeConcini committee in 1988 addressed this problem by proposing tribes secede from the federal administrative system and receive tribal self-governance grants (TSGG), for each tribe "equaling its fair share of the current Federal Indian budget. . . . To further local decision making every TSGG must be provided without program restrictions or categories. Most important, to protect tribal budgets from being eaten away by inflation or the fiscal pressures faced by Congress, the United States will pledge that a tribe's Self-Governance Grant shall be a permanent entitlement with an annual cost-of-living allowance."[9]

The committee's proposals did not become law, and it seems politically unlikely that such open-ended permanent guarantees of federal funds can ever be made. The tribes in the experimental self-governance group do receive relatively unrestricted block grants, but on a temporary basis and only for these few, mostly small, reservations.

A historian friend is fond of quoting a variant of the Golden Rule, "Who has the gold, makes the rules."[10] So long as tribal governments must rely on the federal government for the vast majority of their funding, there must inevitably continue a pattern of federal oversight, hence some degree of "paternalism." The Reagan administration did concern itself with ending tribal dependency through economic development, but that is not inherent in the self-determination policy per se. Reagan's reservation economic commission in fact suggested that Indian government was a problem, not a solution in development. Since 1975, policy makers in general have seemed more interested in self-administration as an immediate goal, apparently content to leave the issue of economic self-sufficiency for the future.

It may be, contrary to Reaganite views, that the one is the key to the other. The Harvard Project on American Indian Economic Development has studied the relation of political development to economic development over a period of years on a number of reservations (Cornell and Kalt 1990, 1998). Overall the researchers' work supports the "therapeutic experience" effect of self-government: "In our work, we cannot find a single case of successful economic development and declining dependence where federal decision makers exercised de facto control over the key development decisions. In every case we can find of sustained economic development on Indian reservations . . . the primary economic decisions are being made by the tribe, not by outsiders" (1998, 13). However, once tribal governments acquire decision-making power, the researchers also suggest, like the Reagan commission, the necessity of giving some of it up, in a "separation of politics from business management" (1998, 7).

Is self-determination synonymous with complete sovereignty? Whatever else federal self-determination policy makers might have had in mind, they probably did not intend the creation of independent ministates. Courts have agreed that Indian governments possess a degree of sovereignty, but they are also clear that it is a limited sovereignty (Pevar 2002, 87). There is no language in the self-determination legislation suggesting any fundamental change in this federal-Indian relation. But in Indian country, some have tended to conflate the self-administration concept with aspirations of complete tribal sovereignty, even of independent Indian statehood. On such emerging assertions of Indian sovereignty, James A. Clifton rather sardonically notes, "Many Indians today are striving to convert ethnicity into nationality. The aim is to carve part of the territories of the United States and Canada into several hundred petty states, so many miniature Indian Monacos and Liechtensteins" (Clifton 1989, 25).[11]

Although there may be some moral logic in the desire for the restoration of pre-Columbian independence, politically and economically, it is probably unrealistic. David E. Wilkins and K. Tsianina Lomawaima ask, "Are tribes today unlimited sovereigns? Certainly not. The political realities of relations with the federal government, relations with state and local governments, competing jurisdictions, complicated local histories, circumscribed land bases, and overlapping citizenships all constrain their sovereignty" (2001, 5). Charles Wilkinson notes, "To be sure, the actual extent of tribal power is less than that of the federal government and the states," but "scores of tribes have actual real-world legal, political and economic power equal to or greater than that of large rural county governments" (2005, 249).

Cherokee historian R. David Edmunds usefully and realistically observed, "There are many definitions of sovereignty in Indian America. It seems to me that the majority of Indians mean 'the maximum amount of self-control for the Indian people under the existing system' when they use this term" (Philp 1986, 290). This is consistent with the 1975 act, which echoes the OEO "maximum feasible participation of the poor" language, by calling for "maximum Indian participation" (Prucha 2000, 275).[12] Just what that maximum might be is obviously a continuum rather than a single fixed point. At any given moment, not all tribes will have achieved the same amount, and some will probably always have more or less than others.

Bee and others have also pointed out that "tribal sovereignty and the federal trust responsibility remain logically and operationally contradictory" (1992, 140). Esber, for example, has suggested on the one hand that "self-determination cannot be accomplished by a policy decision of a dominant government: it can only be achieved by disempowerment of the dominant government and recognition of the genuine sovereignty of the other"; but on the other hand, he suggests permanent dependency. "Along with the trust obligation, the federal government must view its own financial debt as a payment in perpetuity for the privilege that Indian people granted in treaties" (1992, 222). Indian leaders often seem similarly rhetorically (and actually) torn between the pursuit of the freedom of sovereignty and maintenance of the paternalistic protections and funds of the federal trust relationship.

Ultimately, the degree of Indian sovereignty is in the hands of Congress, not the tribes, and the self-determination policy has not changed that. Under existing U.S. law, as Stephen L. Pevar notes, "Congress has *plenary power*—full and complete power—over all Indian tribes, their governments, their members and their property. As the Supreme Court recently stated: 'Congress possesses plenary power over Indian affairs, including the power to modify or eliminate tribal rights,' and Congress can assist or destroy an Indian tribe as it sees fit" (Pevar 2002, 59). Others have noted this precarious situation: "Indian and Alaska Native tribes lack any real, protectable right to exist under the laws of the United States. They exist only at the sufferance or will of the United States Congress" (Coulter 1989, 38).

Some have accordingly suggested the tribes must go outside the U.S. political system and have recourse to international law for protection of indigenous rights (Anaya 2003; Coulter 1989; G. Morris 2003). These commentators and others generally refer to Article 3 of the *United Nations Draft Declaration on the Rights of Indigenous Peoples,* which says, "Indigenous peoples have the right of self-determination. By virtue of that right they freely determine their political status and freely pursue their economic, social and cultural development" (Grounds, Tinker, and Wilkins 2003, 326). The self-determination legislation does not specifically endorse or recognize this international draft statement, nor does any other U.S. legislation (Nesper 2004, 317). For the foreseeable future, in one way or another, the tribes are likely to remain integrated into our overall political system rather than standing outside of it.

By the mid-nineties, whatever its problems, self-determination was the only Indian policy under serious discussion; for those dissatisfied, there was no viable alternative on the table. Despite widespread dissatisfaction with implementation, the critics of the idea of self-determination per se are few and far between.[13] It may well be that the symbolic success of the self-determination policy is sufficient to keep it politically viable for some time to come. Termination has been repudiated, tribes have the hope of managing their own affairs, if not the full reality. It is a seemingly benign policy that politicians can point to with pride—it shows heart.

Notes

Introduction

Epigraph source: "Remarks and a Question and Answer Session with the Students and Faculty at Moscow University, May 31, 1988," *Public Papers of the Presidents of the United States: Ronald Reagan, 1981–1989* (Washington, D.C.: GPO, 1982–1991), 691.

1. Much of the research in this book is based on documents in the various presidential libraries. Those of President Clinton are not yet available, hence the cutoff date of this book's coverage.

2. The best, indeed the only, comprehensive history of federal Indian policy is the two-volume work *The Great Father*, by Francis Paul Prucha (1984).

3. Note also John Wayne on the professorate: "You professors kiss ass for years to get a Ph.D. and tenure. Then you spend the rest of your life trying to change the values of eighteen-year-olds. How pathetic!" (Roberts and Olson 1995, 503).

4. To save the reader time in the library, where possible I cite the compilation *Documents of United States Indian Policy* (Prucha 2000) for historical documents.

5. Page 12, "The History of Federal Indian Policy in Relation to the Development of Indian Communities," *Report and Recommendations*, Chinle Agency Community Development Seminar, May 25–28, 1969, pp. 19–33, Spicer Papers, Arizona State Museum Archives, Tucson.

6. "Home rule" was a phrase commonly used in the context of decolonization, as in Irish home rule or home rule for India.

7. Remarkably, opponents of Collier's "socialist" ideas for Indians included the Nazi propaganda machine (see Townsend 2000, 31).

8. My students always seem to understand when I compare the IRA councils to student governments.

9. Peroff (1982) illustrates how this process played out for the Menominee of Wisconsin.

10. The NCAI supported some aspects of the termination program, particularly the 1946 Indian Claims Commission, which aimed to end Indian financial dependency (Philp 1999, 16).

11. Although Indians benefited from the climate created by the civil rights movement, they never merged their interests with that movement (Lurie 1968, 191; Castile 1998b, 61).

12. Like the Indian New Deal, the OEO was short lived, from 1965 until dismantled during the Nixon administration in 1974.

13. "Special Message to the Congress on the Problems of the American Indian: 'The Forgotten American,' March 6, 1968," *Public Papers of the Presidents of the United States: Lyndon B. Johnson, 1963–1969* (Washington, D.C.: GPO, 1963–[1970/1971]), 336.

14. Page 567 in "Special Message to the Congress on Indian Affairs, July 8, 1970," *Public Papers of the Presidents of the United States: Richard M. Nixon, 1969–1974* (Washington, D.C.: GPO, 1969–[1975/1976]), 565–76.

15. "Address to the Nation on Domestic Programs, August 8, 1969," *Public Papers of the Presidents: Richard M. Nixon,* 237.

Chapter 1. Keeping Faith

1. The NTCA, composed of elected tribal chairs, was formed in 1971 with the support of the Nixon administration (Castile 1998b, 86).

2. Ann S. Ramsay to Landon Butler, "Debrief on Activities/American Indian Desk," November 16, 1976, Jimmy Carter Presidential Library, Atlanta, Georgia.

3. "Draft Statement: Jimmy Carter on American Indians," n.d. (1976?), Domestic Policy Staff Files (Stern), Carter Presidential Library.

4. Ibid.

5. Gerard to President Carter, December 11, 1979, Carter Presidential Library.

6. All commissioners, after Robert L. Bennett was appointed by LBJ in 1966, and all assistant secretaries, including Gerard, were of Indian descent (Castile 1998b, 44).

7. Marilyn G. Haft to Midge Costanza, "Request by Indians for the Appointment of a Special Assistant to the President on Indian Affairs," February 24, 1977, Carter Presidential Library.

8. Berry Crawford to Jack Watson, "IGR Network as a Mechanism for Dealing with Indian Problems," February 22, 1978, Carter Presidential Library.

9. "Indian Education Programs, Statement by the President, July 25, 1978," *Public Papers of the Presidents of the United States: Jimmy Carter, 1977–1980/81* (Washington, D.C.: GPO, 1977–1982), 1336.

10. James T. McIntyre to President Carter, "Letter to the Indian Tribal Chairmen and Some Tribal Organizations Regarding the Department of Education," May 17, 1978, Carter Presidential Library.

11. President Carter to tribal chairs, May 17, 1978, Carter Presidential Library.

12. Eizenstat to Fraser, October 25, 1977, Carter Presidential Library.

13. Harris to Sarah Weddington, assistant to the president for Public Liaison, October 6, 1978, Carter Presidential Library.

14. Cecil Andrus to President Carter, October 19, 1977, Carter Presidential Library.

15. Gerard to executive assistant to the secretary of the interior, "Proposed Presidential Policy Statement on American Indian Policy," October 5, 1977, Carter Presidential Library.

16. Andrus to President Carter, October 19, 1977, Carter Presidential Library.

17. Eizenstat to President Carter, "Andrus Proposal to Prepare an Indian Policy Statement," n.d., Carter Presidential Library.

18. Eliot Cutler to Eizenstat, "Proposed Presidential Review of Indian Policy," January 23, 1978, Carter Presidential Library.

19. Eizenstat to Cutler, January 25, 1978, Carter Presidential Library.

20. Philip Deloria et al. to President Carter, April 13, 1978, Carter Presidential Library.

21. Harris to Weddington, October 6, 1978, Carter Presidential Library.

22. "The State of the Union," January 19, 1978, *Public Papers of the Presidents: Jimmy Carter*, 98.

23. "The State of the Union," January 25, 1979, *Public Papers of the Presidents: Jimmy Carter*, 121.

24. Eizenstat to Kathy Fletcher, "Indian Policy," December 12, 1978, Carter Presidential Library.

25. Richard Pettigrew to McIntyre, October 6, 1978, Carter Presidential Library.

26. An Indian Claims Commission was first created in 1946, in the termination era (Prucha 1984, 1019).

27. Bob Lipshutz to the U.S. attorney general, Griffin B. Bell, "Numerous Claims by Indian Tribes," October 7, 1977, Carter Presidential Library. Henry Martin Jackson, then in the House, had introduced the original claims legislation in 1946 (Prucha 1984, 1019).

28. "Joint Memorandum of Agreement," February 10, 1978, Carter Presidential Library.

29. Carter's comments at the signing ceremony stressed the virtues of negotiation but enunciated no general policy. "Remarks at the Bill Signing Ceremony, October 10, 1980," *Public Papers of the Presidents: Jimmy Carter*, 2176.

30. Carter vetoed a version of the settlement legislation, largely on procedural grounds. "Veto of the Navajo and Hopi Relocation Bill, November 2, 1978," *Public Papers of the Presidents: Jimmy Carter*, 1925.

31. "Federal Water Policy, Message to the Congress," June 6, 1978. *Public Papers of the Presidents: Jimmy Carter*, 1044. On July 12, he sent out a memo to cabinet heads, "Federal and Indian Reserved Water Rights," offering guidance on implementing his policy. Carter Presidential Library.

32. Abourezk to President Carter, April 20, 1978, Carter Presidential Library.

33. McIntyre to Abourezk, May 25, 1978, Carter Presidential Library.

34. Harris to Weddington, October 6, 1978, Carter Presidential Library.

35. Ibid.

36. Emma Gross, in her book *Contemporary Federal Policy Toward American Indians,* has a chapter on "Presidential Initiatives" in which she skips directly from Nixon to Reagan without a section on Carter (Gross 1989, 71).

37. ANILCA was not primarily an "Indian" bill but one that did protect "subsistence" rights of the native peoples on public lands (Catton 1997, 213).

Chapter 2. Congress and Indians

1. I visited the papers of Senator Abourezk at the University of South Dakota, but they contain remarkably little on his role in Indian affairs and are not cited.

2. Robert L. Bee also uses the kamikaze image for Abourezk. "This political kamikaze, a vegetarian in a beef growing state, did not run for reelection" (1992, 159).

3. A very personal account of the AIPRC is found in "Nurturing the Forked Tree" (Thompson 1979).

4. Senate Subcommittee on Indian Affairs, Task Force Four, *Report on Federal, State, and Tribal Jurisdiction: Hearings on the Indian Child Welfare Program* (1974), 93rd Cong, 2nd sess.

5. Stuart Eizenstat and Kathy Fletcher to President Carter, "Enrolled Bill S. 1214—Indian Child Welfare Act of 1978," November 7, 1978, Carter Presidential Library.

6. Eizenstat and Fletcher to President Carter, "Enrolled Bill S. J. Res. 102—American Indian Religious Freedom," August 11, 1978, Carter Presidential Library.

7. Staff recommended Carter sign the bill, saying, "There are no arguments for veto." Eizenstat to President Carter, "Enrolled Bill H.R. 1825—Archaeological Resources Protection Act (Udall)," October 31, 1979, Carter Presidential Library.

8. Ibid. Interestingly, the staff memo recommending approval makes no mention of this national monument issue.

9. Eizenstat to President Carter, "Enrolled Bill S. 1215- Tribally Controlled Community College Assistance Act of 1978," October 18, 1978, Carter Presidential Library.

10. "Tribe" is a term used by anthropologists to label a particular form of social and political complexity in a sequence—band, tribe, chiefdom, state. See Service (1962) for a classic formulation, Johnson and Earle (2000) for a modernized version.

11. "Confederated Tribes of the Siletz Indians of Oregon, Statement on Signing S. 2055 into Law, September 5, 1980," *Public Papers of the Presidents: Jimmy Carter,* 1661.

12. Public Law 95-375, 95th Cong., 2nd sess. (September 18, 1978), *U.S. Statutes at Large* 92 (1978): 712–13.

13. Udall to Aspinall, May 14, 1963, Morris Udall Papers, University of Arizona Library, Tucson.

14. "An Act to provide for the conveyance of certain land of the United States to Pascua Yaqui Association, Inc.," HR 6233, 88th Cong., 2nd Sess. (October 8, 1964).

15. House Committee on Interior and Insular Affairs, *Report to Accompany HR 6612* (March 30, 1978), 95th Cong., 2nd sess., H. Rep. 95-1021.

16. Senate Select Committee on Indian Affairs, *Report to Accompany S 1633* (March 22, 1978), 95th Cong., 2nd sess., S. Rep. 95-719.

17. Ibid.

18. Ibid.

19. S 9003, 95th Cong., 1st sess., *Congressional Record* 123 (June 7, 1977).

20. James T. McIntyre to President Carter, September 12, 1978, Carter Presidential Library.

21. Eizenstat and Fletcher to President Carter, September 15, 1978, Carter Presidential Library.

22. Senate Select Committee on Indian Affairs, *Indian Self-Determination and Education Assistance Act Implementation: Hearings before the Select Committee on Indian Affairs*, 95th Cong., 1st sess. (1977).

23. General Accounting Office, *The Indian Self-Determination Act: Many Obstacles Remain*, Report to the Congress, 95th Cong., 2nd sess. (March 1, 1978).

24. Senate Select Committee on Indian Affairs, *Amend the Indian Self-Determination and Education Assistance Act: Hearings on S 2460*, 95th Cong., 2nd sess. (1978).

25. The issue continued to have legs in Washington State if not in Washington, D.C. As late as 1984 the citizenry of Washington passed a statewide initiative (#456) repudiating Indian fishing rights (Cohen 1986, 186).

26. *Congressional Record* 124, 23134–40.

27. Estimate from Alice Banner, "Indians Complain of Lack of Attention from Carter," *Washington Post*, July 24, 1978 (clipping in Carter Presidential Library). Russell Means, with typical hyperbole, estimates the group at 80,000 (1995, 379).

28. Dennis Banks to President Carter, January 19, 1978, Carter Presidential Library.

29. Eizenstat to President Carter, "Drop by Meeting with Longest Walk Indian Representatives," July 18, 1978, Carter Presidential Library.

30. In December staff indicated the decision was made "some months ago," arguably in the summer of the demonstration. Fletcher to Eizenstat, "Indian Policy," December 12, 1978, Carter Presidential Library.

Chapter 3. Less Is More

1. "Remarks and a Question and Answer Session with the Students and Faculty at Moscow University, May 31, 1988," *Public Papers of the Presidents of the United States: Ronald Reagan, 1981–1988/1989* (Washington, D.C.: GPO, 1982–1991), 691. William Kunstler, as attorney for the three Indians in Moscow—Nilak Butler, Tony Gonzalez, and Russell Redner—attempted to set up a subsequent meeting. There is no indication it ever took place. Kunstler to President Reagan, June 9, 1988, Ronald Reagan Presidential Library, Simi Valley, California.

2. This article by Hertzberg was described as a "hatchet job" by Reagan staff. Edwin L. Harper to Bill Barr, "Indian Policy," November 23, 1982, Reagan Presidential Library. It was also cited as a motive for issuing a presidential policy statement. Elizabeth Dole to William K. Sandler, director of presidential appointments and scheduling, November 24, 1982, Reagan Presidential Library. Reagan in fact made few Westerns and is largely associated with them through his role as host of TV's *Death Valley Days*. (Vaughn 1994, 223, 233) He did make a wartime propaganda film, *For God and Country*, in which he gives his life for an American Indian (Cannon 2003, 68).

3. Lou Cannon (2003, 51) suggests that California Indians had been "eradicated," though he later discusses the Yuki and the Dos Rios Dam (310–13). In a lengthy discussion of Reagan's Interior secretary James Watt, Cannon never mentions Watt's role in Indian affairs (1982, 357–70).

4. Morton C. Blackwell to Rick Neal, "Transfer of Indian Portfolio," February 1, 1983, Reagan Presidential Library. Harper and E. Dole to James A. Baker III and Michael Deaver, "Indian Policy Statement," October 21, 1982, Reagan Presidential Library.

5. Blackwell to E. Dole, "Scheduling Proposal for President's Indian Policy Statement," November 4, 1982, Reagan Presidential Library.

6. Smith to Cabinet Council on Human Resources, "Indian Policy Statement Adopted by the White House Working Group on Indian Policy, August 3, 1982," August 17, 1982, Reagan Presidential Library. "Statement on Indian Policy, January 24, 1983," *Public Papers of the Presidents: Ronald Reagan*, 96–100.

7. "Papago Position Paper on Proposed Budgets and Programs for FY 1982," Ralph L. Sabers to Max H. Norris, Papago chair, June 8, 1981, Reagan Presidential Library.

8. Smith to Hartley F. White, chair, Leach Lake Reservation Business Committee, February 19, 1982, Reagan Presidential Library.

9. "Remarks of Kenneth Smith before the Executive Board Meeting of the National Congress of American Indians," January 25, 1983, Reagan Presidential Library.

10. Blackwell to E. Dole, March 19, 1982, Reagan Presidential Library.

11. Chino to President Reagan, May 7, 1981, Reagan Presidential Library.

12. "Memorandum Returning Without Approval a Bill to Amend the Tribally Controlled Community Colleges Assistance Act of 1978, January 3, 1983," *Public Papers of the Presidents: Ronald Reagan, 7*.

13. "Memorandum Returning Without Approval a Bill to Amend the Education Consolidation and Improvement Act of 1981, January 12, 1983," *Public Papers of the Presidents: Ronald Reagan, 38*.

14. Chino to President Reagan, May 7, 1981, Reagan Presidential Library.

15. Blackwell to E. Dole, May 8, 1981, Reagan Presidential Library.

16. E. Dole to Edwin Meese III, January 20, 1983; Blackwell to E. Dole, March 19, 1982, Reagan Presidential Library.

17. Smith to Chino, July 16, 1981, Reagan Presidential Library.

18. Diana Lozano to E. Dole, "Indian Demonstration: Background and Update," October 19, 1981, Reagan Presidential Library.

19. E. Dole to Martin Anderson, "Indian Demonstration—Follow-Up," November 5, 1981, Reagan Presidential Library.

20. Elmer M. Savilla to President Reagan, October 13, 1981, Reagan Presidential Library.

21. Savilla to Robert Carleson, special assistant to the president for policy development, October 19, 1981; Blackwell to Savilla, November 6, 1981, Reagan Presidential Library.

22. Sabers to Norris, Papago chair, June 8, 1981, Reagan Presidential Library.

23. Theodore C. Kronzko, deputy assistant secretary, Indian affairs, to Alec Garfield, president, California Tribal Chairman's Association, March 2, 1982, Reagan Presidential Library.

24. "Proclamation 5049—American Indian Day, 1983, April 14, 1983." *Public Papers of the Presidents: Ronald Reagan, 536*. "Proclamation 5577—American Indian Week, 1986, November 24, 1986." *Public Papers of the Presidents: Ronald Reagan, 1558–66*.

25. Indian Affairs Working Group Membership List, n.d. [Indicates "Date Established: August 1981."], Reagan Presidential Library.

26. McClaughry to Martin Anderson, "Indian Wars," October 16, 1981, Reagan Presidential Library.

27. McClaughry to Bob Carleson, "Indian Policy Working Group," October 6, 1981, Reagan Presidential Library.

28. Lo Anne Wagner to Carleson, "Status Report—White House Working Group on Indian Affairs," May 4, 1982, Reagan Presidential Library.

29. Smith to Cabinet Council on Human Resources, "Indian Policy Statement Adopted by the White House Working Group on Indian Policy, August 3, 1982," August 17, 1982, Reagan Presidential Library.

30. Ibid.

31. Wagner to Monie Murphy, Presidential Scheduling. "Presidential Release of Indian Policy Statement in Arizona or California," September 30, 1982, Reagan Presidential Library.

32. Barr to Harper, "Need for Quick Action on Indian Policy Statement," October 20, 1982, Reagan Presidential Library.

33. Harper and E. Dole to Baker and Deaver, "Indian Policy Statement," October 21, 1982. Reagan Presidential Library.

34. Robert Nelson, Task Force on Economic Development, Department of the Interior. *Report of the Task Force on Indian Economic Development* (Washington D.C.: Government Printing Office, 1986), 4.

35. "Excerpts from an interview with Secretary of the Interior James G. Watt," Reagan Presidential Library.

36. Harris to President Reagan, January 20, 1983, Reagan Presidential Library.

37. Transcript of *Good Morning America,* January 20, 1983, Reagan Presidential Library.

38. "Remarks of Secretary of the Interior James Watt to the National Congress of American Indians Executive Board, January 25, 1983," Reagan Presidential Library.

39. E. Dole to Meese, Baker, Deaver, "Secretary Watt and Indian Policy," January 20, 1983, Reagan Presidential Library.

40. "Statement on Indian Policy, January 24, 1983," *Public Papers of the Presidents: Ronald Reagan,* 96.

41. Ibid., 97.

42. Ibid.

43. Ibid., 98.

44. Ibid.

45. Ibid.

46. "Executive Order 12401—Presidential Commission on Indian Reservation Economies, January 14, 1983," *Public Papers of the Presidents: Ronald Reagan,* 56.

47. "Statement on Indian Policy, January 24, 1983," *Public Papers of the Presidents: Ronald Reagan,* 99.

48. Ibid., 99.

49. Morris Udall et al. to President Reagan, April 22, 1983, Reagan Presidential Library.

50. "Executive Order 12401—Presidential Commission on Indian Reservation Economies, January 14, 1983," *Public Papers of the Presidents: Ronald Reagan,* 57.

51. Robert Robertson and Ross O. Swimmer, Presidential Commission on Indian Reservation Economies. *Report and Recommendations to the President of the United States* (Washington, D.C.: Government Printing Office, 1984).

52. Ibid., 9–10.

53. Ibid., 25.

54. Ibid., 33–39.

55. Ibid., 32.

56. Ibid., 41.

57. Ibid., 26.

58. Ibid., 32.

59. Morris references the phrase to the Salish Kootenai newspaper *Charkoosta*, but I was unable to find the phrase in the cited issue—November 4, 1987, 16 (25): 1.

60. Robertson and Swimmer, Presidential Commission on Indian Reservation Economies. *Report and Recommendations to the President of the United States*, 41.

61. "Reaganomics" like El Nino has been blamed for almost everything, including punk rock (Watson 1995, 216). In Indian affairs, one author suggests it is responsible for "radioactive colonization" of the reservations (Hanson 2001, 22).

62. McClaughry to Ed Gray, "Ancient Indian Land Claims Settlement Act," February 16, 1982, Reagan Presidential Library.

63. "Message to the House of Representatives Returning Without Approval the Southern Arizona Water Rights Settlement Bill, June 1, 1982," *Public Papers of the Presidents: Ronald Reagan*, 711–12.

64. "Statement on Signing a Bill Relating to Water Rights of the Ak-Chin Indians, October 19, 1984," *Public Papers of the Presidents: Ronald Reagan*, 1580.

65. "Message to the Senate Returning Without Approval the Mashantucket Pequot Indian Claims Settlement Bill, April 5, 1983," *Public Papers of the Presidents: Ronald Reagan*, 498.

66. James C. Miller III to President Reagan, "Enrolled Bill H.R. 2855—Wampanoag Tribal Council of Gay Head, Inc., Indian Claims Settlement Act of 1987," August 16, 1987, Reagan Presidential Library.

67. Miller to President Reagan, "Enrolled Bill H.R. 3554—Klamath Indian Tribe Recognition, Sponsor Rep. Smith (R) Oregon," August 25, 1989, Reagan Presidential Library.

68. Office of the Secretary memorandum, "Indian issue—accomplishments, June 1, 1983," Reagan Presidential Library.

69. In constant dollars, the cuts were actually somewhat greater than most sources note. In constant dollars, the BIA education programs, $417,143,000 in 1982, fell to $329,853,000 in 1989 (CRS 1998, 220).

Chapter 4. Casinos and Investigations

1. Robert Robertson and Ross O. Swimmer, Presidential Commission on Indian Reservation Economies. *Report and Recommendations to the President of the United States* (Washington, D.C.: Government Printing Office, 1984).

2. Robert Nelson, Task Force on Economic Development, Department of the Interior. *Report of the Task Force on Indian Economic Development.* (Washington D.C.: Government Printing Office, 1986).

3. Ibid., 2.

4. Ibid., 20.

5. Ibid.

6. As noted above, this small increase is a loss in constant dollars (CRS 1998).

7. Un-Reaganite observers have also endorsed the necessity for Indian control over Indian resources as a key to economic development (*The Economist* 1996; Cornell and Kalt 1990).

8. U.S. Senate, *A Report of the Special Committee on Investigations of the Select Committee on Indian Affairs* (November 20, 1989), 101st Cong., 1st sess., 225.

9. Ibid., 213.

10. Ibid., 214.

11. Ibid., 215.

12. Tammany modeled its organization of braves, sachems, and wiskinskys on its vision of American Indian society, hence Tammany Indians (Allen 1993, 6).

13. U.S. Senate, *A Report of the Special Committee on Investigations of the Select Committee on Indian Affairs* (November 20, 1989), 101st Cong., 1st sess., 182.

14. President Reagan to MacDonald, n.d., Reagan Presidential Library. "Proclamation 4954—National Navajo Code Talkers Day, July 28, 1982," *Public Papers of the Presidents: Ronald Reagan*, 980.

15. Morton Blackwell to Elizabeth Dole, March 19, 1982, Reagan Presidential Library.

16. Goldwater to Max Friedersdorf, April 27, 1981; Goldwater to E. Dole, September 30, 1982, Reagan Presidential Library.

17. U.S. Senate, *A Report of the Special Committee on Investigations of the Select Committee on Indian Affairs* (November 20, 1989), 101st Cong., 1st sess., 181.

18. Ibid., 194.

19. Ibid., 197.

20. In 2001 MacDonald's sentence was commuted after seven years by outgoing President Clinton. ("Peter MacDonald Free after Seven Years," *Indian Country Today*, January 31, 2001).

21. Nelson, Task Force on Economic Development, *Report of the Task Force on Indian Economic Development*, 20.

22. James C. Miller III, OMB Director, to President Reagan. "Memorandum for the President, October 11, 1988," Reagan Presidential Library.

23. Chino to President Reagan, October 5, 1988, Reagan Presidential Library.

24. Miller to President Reagan, "Memorandum for the President, Enrolled Bill S. 555—Indian Gaming Regulatory Act," October 11, 1988, Reagan Presidential Library.

25. Interestingly, given the importance of the bill, there was no accompanying explanatory signing statement.

26. National Gambling Impact Study Commission, "Native American Tribal Gambling," 6-1, *Final Report*, www.ngisc.gov/research/nagaming/html (accessed June 18, 1999). At the time of this writing, the gross amount is estimated at $18.5 billion. "Indian Casino Take Is Nearly Twice Nevada's," *Arizona Daily Star*, February 16, 2005, A5. See also "Tribal Government Gaming: The Native American Success Story," National Indian Gaming Association (2004), Indiangaming.org/NIGA_econ_impact_2004.pdf (accessed July 9, 2005).

27. After repeatedly rejecting gaming, the Navajo approved it in November 2004. John Stearn, "Navajos Seek Gaming Director: Tribe Prepares to Launch 1st Casino," *Arizona Republic*, March 4, 2005, D1.

28. NGIS Commission, "Native American Tribal Gambling," 6-2, *Final Report*, www.ngisc.gov/research/nagaming/html (accessed June 18, 1999).

29. *Time* magazine published an exposé: Donald L. Barlett and James B. Steele, "Wheel of Misfortune: Special Report on Indian Casinos," December 16, 2002, 42–58.

30. Some interesting bills failed. A proposal to create an American Indian development bank was one of these. For its legislative saga, see Pottinger (1991).

31. Senate Select Committee on Indian Affairs, *Indian Self-Determination and Educational Assistance Act: Hearings on Recommendations for Strengthening the Indian Self-Determination Act, Public Law 93-638* (April 22, 1987), 100th Cong., 1st sess.

32. Miller to President Reagan, "Enrolled Bill H.R. 1233—Indian Self-Determination Amendments of 1988," September 19, 1988, Reagan Presidential Library.

33. Ibid.

34. "Statement on Signing the Indian Self-Determination and Education Assistance Act Amendments of 1988, October 5, 1988," *Public Papers of the Presidents: Ronald Reagan*, 1284.

35. "Memorandum Returning Without Approval the Indian Health Care Amendments of 1984, October 19, 1984." *Public Papers of the Presidents: Ronald Reagan*, 1584–85.

36. Draft "Memorandum of Disapproval," in "Memorandum for the President, Enrolled Bill H.R. 5261—Indian Health Care Amendments of 1988," November 18, 1988, Ronald Reagan Presidential Library.

37. Draft "Statement by the President," in "Memorandum for the President, Enrolled Bill H.R. 3927—Indian Housing Act of 1988," June 23, 1988, Ronald Reagan Presidential Library.

38. *Public Papers of the Presidents: Ronald Reagan*, 749

39. Cristina L. Bach to Reverend William Wong, July 25, 1988, Reagan Presidential Library.

40. "Statement by Ross Swimmer, Assistant Secretary, Indian Affairs, Regarding President Reagan's Recent Remarks About Indians," June 10, 1988, Reagan Presidential Library.

41. "Statement by Assistant to the President for Press Relations Fitzwater on the President's Meeting With American Indian Leaders," December 12, 1988, *Public Papers of the Presidents: Ronald Reagan*, 1988. There is what amounts to a script prepared for this meeting. Nancy J. Risque to Reagan, December 9, 1988, Reagan Presidential Library.

Chapter 5. A Kinder, Gentler Indian Policy?

1. "George Bush on Native Americans," n.d., Bush Presidential Library, College Station, Texas.
2. "Dear Indian Leader," October 30, 1988, Bush Presidential Library.
3. Ibid.
4. "Nomination of Eddie F. Brown to be an Assistant Secretary of Interior," April 13, 1989, *Public Papers of the Presidents: George Bush, 1989–1993* (Washington, D.C.: GPO, 1990–[1994]), 415–16.
5. Mary McClure to agency/department officials, "White House Native American Interagency Task Force," June 21, 1989, Bush Presidential Library.
6. DeConcini et al. to President Bush, "Re: American Indian Policy," February 23, 1989, Bush Presidential Library.
7. Richard Nixon to DeConcini et al., January 26, 1989, Bush Presidential Library.
8. LaDonna Harris to President Bush, February 8, 1990; John J. Rhodes to John Sununu, April 3, 1990, Bush Presidential Library.
9. Debra Anderson to LaDonna Harris, March 1, 1990, Bush Presidential Library.
10. Quoted in "Remarks of Mary McClure before the NCSL Task Force on State-Tribal Relations, December 12, 1990," Bush Presidential Library.
11. "Summary of Presidential Meeting with Tribal Chairman, April 17, 1991," Bush Presidential Library.
12. "Statement Reaffirming the Government-to-Government Relationship Between the Federal Government and Indian Tribal Governments," June 14, 1991, Public Papers of the Presidents: George Bush, 622–23.
13. LaDonna Harris to President Bush, July 3, 1991, Bush Presidential Library.
14. The Reagan administration had in fact also encouraged the contracting process.
15. He pocket vetoed the Indian Preference Act of 1990 and the 1992 Amendments to the Mississippi Sioux Judgment Fund.
16. "Statement on Signing a Bill Amending Indian Laws," May 24, 1990, *Public Papers of the Presidents: George Bush, 725*
17. "Statement on Signing the Bill Reauthorizing Native American Higher Education Assistance," October 30, 1990, *Public Papers of the Presidents: George Bush, 1497.*
18. "Statement on Signing the Native American Languages Act of 1992," October 26, 1992, *Public Papers of the Presidents: George Bush.*
19. See www.nativehawaiians.com for the present status of recognition bills.
20. "Statement on Signing the Puyallup Tribe of Indians Settlement Act of 1989," June 21, 1989, *Public Papers of the Presidents: George Bush, 771–72.*
21. "Statement on Signing the Fort Hall Indian Water Rights Act of 1990," November 16, 1990, *Public Papers of the Presidents: George Bush.*

22. Indian Nations at Risk Task Force, *Indian Nations at Risk: Solutions for the 1990s* (Washington, D.C.: Department of Education, 1991).

23. Rep. Ben Campbell et al. to President Bush, June 27, 1989, Bush Presidential Library.

24. "The Arthur F. Hawkins-Robert T. Stafford Elementary and Secondary School Improvement Act of 1988," Public Law 100-297, 100th Cong., 2nd sess. (April 28, 1988).

25. Buck Martin, Indian Nations at Risk Task Force, *The Final Report of the White House Conference on Indian Education*. 2 vols. (Washington, D.C.: Department of Education, May 1992).

26. "Letter to Congressional Leaders Transmitting the Report of the White House Conference on Indian Education," October 9, 1992, *Public Papers of the Presidents: George Bush*, 1785.

27. "Response to the Recommendations of the Report on the White House Conference on Indian Education," Bush Presidential Library.

28. Gorton to John Sununu, "Tribally Controlled Colleges Reauthorization," October 17, 1990, Bush Presidential Library.

29. "Statement on Signing the Bill Reauthorizing Native American Higher Education Assistance, October 30, 1990," *Public Papers of the Presidents: George Bush*, 1598.

30. "Statement on Signing the Native American Languages Act of 1992," October 26, 1992, *Public Papers of the Presidents: George Bush*, 1497.

31. U.S. Senate, *A Report of the Special Committee on Investigations of the Select Committee on Indian Affairs* (November 20, 1989), 101st Cong., 1st sess., 15.

32. "Tribal Leaders Skeptical of BIA Restructuring," *Washington Post*, October 1, 1990 (clipping in Bush Presidential Library).

33. Quoted in "Resentments Still Fresh as Indians Meet with Lujan," *New York Times*, September 30, 1990 (clipping in Bush Presidential Library).

34. Richard Darman to President Bush, "Enrolled Bill H. R. 3394—Tribal Self-Governance Demonstration Project Act," November 27, 1991, Bush Presidential Library.

35. "Statement on Signing the National Museum of the American Indian Act," November 28, 1989, *Public Papers of the Presidents: George Bush*, 1598.

36. Although the law was signed in 1989, the museum was not actually opened to the public until September 21, 2004.

37. Geoffrey A. Clark has wryly observed, "Anthropologists are an even weaker political constituency than Indians" (1999, 46).

38. Some have even suggested its problems rise to the level of being unconstitutional (Parsley 1993).

39. Campbell apparently adopted the name "Nighthorse" when he began his jewelry career (Viola 2002, 171).

40. The NCAI president wrote to Bush objecting to the use of the term "Indian country" by the military in the Gulf War, a sign perhaps that Indian ethnic

sensitivity had been abraded in the lead-in to Columbus Day. Franklin D. Ducheneaux to President Bush, February 19, 1991, Bush Presidential Library.

41. Memo from Harjo to Friends of the 1992 Alliance, November 26, 1991,
Bush Presidential Library.

42. "Native American Indian Heritage Month, 1991: A Proclamation," October 30, 1991, Bush Presidential Library.

43. "Year of the American Indian, 1992: A Proclamation," March 2, 1992, Bush
Presidential Library.

Epilogue

1. In addition to those discussed in this book, both presidents Bill Clinton
and George W. Bush have issued brief endorsement statements. "Remarks to Native American and Native Alaskan Tribal Leaders, April 29, 1994," *Public Papers
of the Presidents: William J. Clinton, 1993–[2001]* (Washington, D.C.: GPO, 1994–
[2001/2002]), 801. "Memorandum on Government-to-Government Relationship
with Tribal Governments, September 23, 2004." *Public Papers of the Presidents:
George W. Bush, 2001–* (Washington, D.C.: GPO, 2003–), 2106.

2. *Commemorating the 30th Anniversary of the Policy of Self-Determination*, S.
Res. 277 (June 27, 2000), 106th Cong., 2nd sess. Despite the resolution's bipartisan
sponsorship, Nixon is given sole credit as the originator of the policy, ignoring
the earlier 1968 statement of LBJ.

3. The backlash in 1977, described in chapter 2, was a generalized opposition
to all "special" status for American Indians, not focused on the self-determination policy per se (Prucha 1994, 422). Senator Slade Gorton did mount unsuccessful challenges to self-governance and other Indian issues after his reelection in
1994, but not only were they unsupported, they lie outside the temporal coverage
of this book (Wilkins and Lomawaima 2001, 240).

4. "Statement of Bonnie Cohen," House Subcommittee on Native American
Affairs of the Committee on Natural Resources, *Oversight Hearing on the Implementation of the Indian Self-Determination Act, and the Development of Regulations following Passage of the 1988 Amendments* (July 29, 1995) 103rd Cong., 2nd
sess., serial no. 103–5.

5. Ibid., 1.

6. "Statement of Hon. John McCain, U.S. Senator for Arizona," ibid., 1, 5.

7. There is a certain irony in the bureau-bashing by tribal representatives
in these hearings. Because of the operation of Indian preference, by this point
virtually all the high-level BIA bureaucrats defending the agency were Indians
(Novack 1990).

8. There are remarkably few general examinations of modern reservation
economies. One excellent recent study of the Lakota reservations Pine Ridge and
Rosebud is Pickering's *Lakota Culture, World Economy* (Pickering 2000). A more
general discussion by the same author is found in Pickering (2004).

9. U.S. Senate, *A Report of the Special Committee on Investigations of the Select Committee on Indian Affairs* (November 20, 1989), 101st Cong., 1st sess., 18–19.

10. Thomas Edwards, emeritus professor of history, Whitman College.

11. The comparison to Monaco and Liechtenstein is obviously meant to be humorous, but it is not as far-fetched as first thought suggests. Monaco, with a "native" population of just over five thousand and a territory of under two square kilometers, and Liechtenstein, with 160 square kilometers and a citizen population of less than twenty thousand, are both smaller in scale than many reservations (Duursma 1996, 261, 147).

12. George Esber in fact suggests of the Self-Determination Act, "A more appropriate name for the policy would have been the Indian Participation Act" (1992, 221).

13. See Tom Flanagan, *First Nations? Second Thoughts* (2000), for an example, albeit focused primarily on Canada, not the United States.

References Cited

Abourezk, James G.
 1989 *Advise and Dissent: Memoirs of South Dakota and the Senate.* Chicago: Lawrence Hills Books.

Achuleta, Margaret, Brenda J. Child, and K. Tsianina Lomawaima
 2000 Introduction. In *Away from Home: American Indian Boarding School Experiences,* ed. Margaret Achuleta, Brenda J. Child, and K. Tsianina Lomawaima. Phoenix: Heard Museum.

AIPRC [American Indian Policy Review Commission]
 1977 *American Indian Policy Review Commission, Final Report, May 17, 1977.* Washington, D.C.: Government Printing Office.

Allen, Oliver E.
 1993 *The Tiger: The Rise and Fall of Tammany Hall.* Reading, Mass.: Addison-Wesley.

Ambrose, Stephen E.
 1991 *Ruin and Recovery, 1973–1990.* Vol. 3 of *Nixon.* New York: Simon and Schuster.

Anaya, S. James
 2003 "International Law and U.S. Trust Responsibility toward Native Americans." In *Native Voices: American Indian Identity and Resistance,* ed. Richard A. Grounds, George E. Tinker, and David E. Wilkins, 155–86. Lawrence: University Press of Kansas.

Anders, Gary C.
 1998 "Indian Gaming: Financial and Regulatory Issues." *Annals of the American Academy of Political and Social Science* 556:98–108.

Anderson, Terry H.
 1995 *The Movement and the Sixties: Protest in America from Greensboro to Wounded Knee.* New York: Oxford University Press.

Andrus, Cecil, and Joel Connelly
 1998 *Cecil Andrus: Politics Western Style.* Seattle: Sasquatch Books.

Ashley, Jeffrey S., and Secody J. Hubbard
 2004 *Negotiated Sovereignty: Working to Improve Tribal-State Relations.* Westport, Conn.: Praeger.

Barker, Joanne
    2003   "Indian U.S.A." *Wicazo Sa Review* 18 (1):25–81.

Barlett, Donald L., and James B. Steele
    2002   "Wheel of Misfortune." Special Report: Indian Casinos. December 16, 42–58.

Barringer, Sandra K.
    1997   "Indian Activism and the American Indian Movement: A Bibliographical Essay." *American Indian Culture and Research Journal* 21 (4):217–050.

Baylor, Timothy John
    1994   "Modern Warriors: Mobilization and Decline of the American Indian Movement (AIM), 1968-1979." PhD dissertation, University of North Carolina.

Bee, Robert L.
    1979   "To Get Something for the People: The Predicament of the American Indian Leader." *Human Organization* 38:239–47.
    1982   *The Politics of American Indian Policy.* Cambridge, Mass.: Schenkman Publishing.
    1990   "The Predicament of the Native American Leader: A Second Look." *Human Organization* 49 (1):56–63.
    1992   "Riding the Paper Tiger." In *State and Reservation: New Perspectives on Federal Indian Policy,* ed. George Castile and Robert Bee, 410–30. Tucson: University of Arizona Press.

Beinart, Peter
    1999   "Lost Tribes." *Lingua Franca* 9 (4): 33–41.

Benedict, Jeff
    2000   *Without Reservation: The Making of America's Most Powerful Indian Tribe and Foxwoods, The World's Largest Casino.* New York: Harper Collins.

Bernstein, Alison
    1991   *American Indians and World War II: Toward a New Era in Indian Affairs.* Norman: University of Oklahoma Press.

Biolsi, Thomas
    1992   *Organizing the Lakota: The Political Economy of the New Deal on the Pine Ridge and Rosebud Reservations.* Tucson: University of Arizona Press.
    2001   *Deadliest Enemies: Law and the Making of Race Relations on and off Rosebud Reservation.* Berkeley: University of California Press.
    2004   "Political and Legal Status ('Lower 48' States)." In *A Companion to the Anthropology of American Indians,* ed. Thomas Biolsi, 231–47. Oxford: Blackwell Publishing.

Bourne, Peter G.
    1997   *Jimmy Carter: A Comprehensive Biography from Plains to Postpresidency.* A Lisa Drew Book. New York: Scribner.

Brand, Stewart
  1988   "Indians and the Counterculture, 1960s–1970s." In *History of Indian-White Relations,* vol. 4 of *Handbook of North American Indians,* ed. Wilcomb E. Washburn, 570–72. Washington, D.C.: Smithsonian Institution.

Bray, Tamara L.
  2001   "American Archaeologists and Native Americans: A Relationship Under Construction." In *The Future of the Past: Archaeologists, Native Americans, and Repatriation,* ed. Tamara L. Bray, 1–8. New York: Garland.

Brosnan, Dolores
  1996   "Indian Policy, Indian Gambling, and the Future of Tribal Economic Development." *American Review of Public Administration* 26 (2):213–v29.

Burt, Larry W.
  1982   *Tribalism in Crisis: Federal Indian Policy, 1953–1961.* Albuquerque: University of New Mexico Press.

Burton, Lloyd
  1991   *American Indian Water Rights and the Limits of Law.* Lawrence: University Press of Kansas.

Bush, George
  1999   *All the Best, George Bush: My Life in Letters and Other Writings.* New York: Scribner.
  2001   *Heartbeat: George Bush in His Own Words.* New York: Scribner.

Bush, George, with Victor Gold
  1987   *Looking Forward.* New York: Doubleday.

Califano, Joseph A., Jr.
  1981   *Governing America: An Insider's Report from the White House and Cabinet.* New York: Simon and Schuster.

Campisi, Jack
  1990   "The New England Tribes and Their Quest for Justice." In *The Pequots in Southern New England: The Fall and Rise of an American Indian Nation,* ed. Laurence M. Hauptman and James D. Wherry, 179–93. Norman: University of Oklahoma Press.
  1991   *The Mashpee Indians: Tribe on Trial.* Syracuse, N.Y.: Syracuse University Press.

Cannon, Lou
  1982   *Reagan.* New York: Putnam and Sons.
  1991   *President Reagan: The Role of a Lifetime.* New York: Simon Schuster.
  2003   *Governor Reagan: His Rise to Power.* New York: Public Affairs Press.

Carson, Donald W., and James W. Johnson
  2001   *Mo: The Life and Times of Morris K. Udall.* Tucson: University of Arizona Press.

Carter, Jimmy
1982   *Keeping Faith: Memoirs of a Presidency.* New York: Bantam.
Castile, George Pierre
1968   "The Community School at Rough Rock." Master's thesis, University of Arizona.
1974   "Federal Indian Policy and the Sustained Enclave: An Anthropological Perspective." *Human Organization* 33 (3):219–28.
1978   "The Headless Horsemen: Recapitating the Beheaded Community." *The Indian Historian* 11 (3):38–45.
1979   *North American Indians: An Introduction to the Chichimeca.* New York: McGraw-Hill.
1982   "Land Lust to Fish Lust: Resource Competition and Indian Policy in the Pacific Northwest." Paper presented at the American Anthropological Association, Washington, D.C.
1985   "Indian Fighting for Fun and Profit: Sources of Indian Policy in the Pacific Northwest." Paper presented at the Society for Applied Anthropology, Washington, D.C.
1988   "The Miskito and the 'Spanish': A Historical Perspective on the Ethnogenesis and Persistence of a People." In *Central America: Historical Perspectives on the Contemporary Crises,* ed. Ralph Lee Woodward, 131–46. Westport, Conn.: Greenwood Press.
1992   "Indian Sign: Hegemony and Symbolism in Federal Indian Policy." In *State and Reservation: New Perspectives on Federal Indian Policy,* ed. George Castile and Robert Bee, 165–86. Tucson: University of Arizona Press.
1996   "The Commodification of Indian Identity." *American Anthropologist* 98 (4):743–49.
1998a   "Maybe We Should Not Have Humored Them: Federal Indian Policy in the Reagan Administration." Paper presented at the American Anthropological Association, Philadelphia.
1998b   *To Show Heart: Native American Self-Determination and Federal Indian Policy, 1960–1975.* Tucson: University of Arizona Press.
1999   "Les Jeux Sont Faits: Federal Indian Policy and Indian Gaming." Paper presented at the American Society for Ethnohistory, Mashantucket, Connecticut.
2002   "Yaquis, Edward H. Spicer, and Federal Indian Policy." *Journal of the Southwest* 44 (4):385–435.
2004   "Federal Indian Policy and Anthropology." In *A Companion to the Anthropology of American Indians.* ed. Thomas Biolsi, 268–83. Oxford: Blackwell Publishing.
Catton, Theodore
1997   *Inhabited Wilderness: Indians, Eskimos, and National Parks in Alaska.* Albuquerque: University of New Mexico Press.

Cawley, R. McGreggor

1986   "James Watt and the Environmentalists: A Clash of Ideologies." *Policy Studies Journal* 14 (2):244–54.

Cheek, Annetta L.

1991   "Protection of Archaeological Resources on Public Lands: History of the Archaeological Resources Protection Act." In *Protecting the Past,* ed. George S. Smith and John E. Erenhard, 33–44. Boca Raton, Fla.: CRC Press.

Clark, Geoffrey A.

1999   "NAGPRA, Science and the Demon-Haunted World." *Skeptical Inquirer* 23 (3):44–45.

Clifton, James A.

1989   "Alternative Identities and Cultural Frontiers." In *Being and Becoming Indian: Biographical Studies of North American Frontiers,* ed. James A. Clifton, 1–37. Chicago: Dorsey Press.

Cobb, Daniel M.

1998   "Philosophy of an Indian War: Indian Community Action in the Johnson Administration's War on Indian Poverty,1964–1968." *American Indian Quarterly and Research Journal* 22:71–102.

Cohen, Fay G.

1986   *Treaties on Trial: The Continuing Controversy over Northwest Coast Indian Fishing Rights.* Seattle: University of Washington Press.

Cohen, Felix

1942   *Handbook of Federal Indian Law.* Washington, D.C.: Government Printing Office.

Collier, John

1935   "A Birdseye View of Indian Policy Historic and Contemporary." Submitted to the Subcommittee of the Appropriation Committee of the House of Representatives, December 30, 1935. Tucson: University of Arizona Library Microfiche.

1947   *The Indians of the Americas.* New York: Norton and Co.

1963   *From Every Zenith: A Memoir and Some Essays on Life and Thought.* Denver: Sage Press.

Collins, Robert B., and Mark P. Michel

1985   "Preserving the Past: Origins of the Archaeological Protection Act of 1979." *American Archaeology* 5 (2):84–89.

Conkin, Paul Keith

1986   *Big Daddy from the Pedenales: Lyndon Baines Johnson.* Boston: Twayne.

Conlan, Timothy

1988   *New Federalism: Intergovernmental Reform from Nixon to Reagan.* Washington, D.C.: The Brookings Institution.

Cook, Samuel R.

    1994   "What is Indian Self-Determination?" *Red Ink* 3 (1):23–26.

    1996   "Ronald Reagan's Indian Policy in Retrospect: Economic Crisis and Political Irony." *Policy Studies Journal* 24 (1):11–26.

Cooper, Mary H.

    1996   "Native Americans' Future." *Congressional Quarterly* 6 (26):601–24.

Cornell, Stephen

    1988   *The Return of the Native: American Indian Political Resurgence.* New York: Oxford University Press.

Cornell, Stephen, and Joseph P. Kalt

    1990   "Pathways from Poverty: Economic Development and Institution Building on American Indian Reservations." *American Indian Culture and Research Journal* 14 (1):89–115.

    1998   "Sovereignty and Nation Building: The Development Challenge in Indian Country Today." *American Indian Culture and Research Journal* 22 (3):187–214.

Coulter, Robert T.

    1989   "Present and Future Status of American Indian Nations and Tribes." In *Indian Self Governance: Perspectives on the Political Status of Indian Nations in the United States of America,* ed. Carol J. Minugh, Glenn T. Morris, and Rudolph Ryeser, 37–48. Kenmore, Wash.: Center for World Indigenous Studies.

Cowger, Thomas W.

    1999   *The National Congress of American Indians: The Founding Years.* Lincoln: University of Nebraska Press.

Cozzetto, Dona A., and Brent W. Larocque

    1996   "Compulsive Gambling in the Indian Community: A North Dakota Case Study." *American Indian Culture and Research Journal* 20 (1):73–86.

CRS [Congressional Research Service]

    1998   "Indian Related Federal Spending Trends, FY 1975–1999." Washington D.C.: Library of Congress.

Dahl, Kathleen A.

    1994   "The Battle Over Termination on the Colville Indian Reservation." *American Indian Culture and Research Journal* 18 (1):29–53.

Daily, David W.

    2004   *Battle for the BIA: G.E.E. Lindquist and the Missionary Crusade against John Collier.* Tucson: University of Arizona Press.

Dean, S. Bobo, and Joseph H. Webster

    2000   "Contract Support Funding and the Federal Policy of Indian Tribal Self-Determination." *Tulsa Law Journal* 36 (2):349–80.

Deloria, Vine, Jr.

    1974   *Behind the Trail of Broken Treaties: An Indian Declaration of Independence.* Austin: University of Texas Press.

1984   "Congress in Its Wisdom." In *The Aggressions of Civilization: Federal Indian Policy Since the 1880s*, ed. Sandra L. Cadwalader and Vine Deloria Jr., 105–30. Philadelphia: Temple University Press.

2001   "The Perpetual Education Report." In *Power and Place: Indian Education in America*, ed. Vine Deloria Jr. and Daniel R. Wildcat, 151–61. Golden, Colo.: Fulcrum.

Deloria, Vine, Jr., ed.

2002   *The Indian Reorganization Act: Congresses and Bills*. Norman: University of Oklahoma Press.

Deloria, Vine, Jr., and Clifford Lytle

1984   *The Nations Within: The Past and Future of American Indian Sovereignty*. New York: Pantheon.

Detlefsen, Robert R.

1991   *Civil Rights Under Reagan*. San Francisco: Institute for Contemporary Studies.

Duffy, Michael, and Dan Goodgame

1992   *Marching in Place: The Status Quo Presidency of George Bush*. New York: Simon and Schuster.

Dumbrell, John

1993   *The Carter Presidency: A Re-evaluation*. Manchester: Manchester University Press.

Duursma, Jorri

1996   *Fragmentation and the International Relations of Micro-States: Self-Determination and Statehood*. Cambridge; New York: Cambridge University Press.

Economist, The

1996   "How to Succeed, How to Fail: Indian Reservations." *The Economist* (US) 339 (7960):25.

Eizenstat, Stuart E.

1997   "President Carter, the Democratic Party, and the Making of Domestic Policy." In *The Presidency and Domestic Policies of Jimmy Carter*, ed. Herbert D. Rosenbaum and Alexej Uginsky, 3–16. Westport, Conn.: Greenwood Press.

Esber, George

1992   "Shortcomings of the Indian Self-Determination Policy." In *State and Reservation: New Perspectives on Federal Indian policy*. ed. George Castile and Robert Bee, 212–23. Tucson: University of Arizona Press.

FCNL [Friends Committee on National Legislation]

1991   "The President Speaks to National Leaders—Government to Government." *Indian Report* 1:40.

Ferguson, T. J.

1996   "Native Americans and the Practice of Archaeology." *Annual Reviews in Anthropology* 25:63–79.

Fink, Gary, and Hugh Davis Graham, eds.

    1998   *The Carter Presidency: Policy Choices in the Post–New Deal Era*. Lawrence: University Press of Kansas.

Fireman, Janet

    1995   "Ronald Reagan and the Mythic West." *Journal of the West* 34 (2):91–97.

Fixico, Donald Lee

    1986   *Termination and Relocation: Federal Indian Policy, 1945–1960*. Albuquerque: University Of New Mexico Press.

Flanagan, Tom

    2000   *First Nations? Second Thoughts*. Montreal: McGill-Queen's University.

Force, Roland W.

    1999   *Politics and the Museum of the American Indian: The Heye and the Mighty*. Honolulu: Mechas Press.

Fowler, Loretta

    1982   *Arapahoe Politics, 1851–1978: Symbols in Crises of Authority*. Lincoln: University of Nebraska Press.

    2002   *Tribal Sovereignty and the Historical Imagination: Cheyenne Arapaho Politics*. Lincoln: University of Nebraska Press.

Gabriel, Kathryn

    1996   *Gambler Way: Indian Gaming in Mythology, History, and Archaeology in North America*. Boulder, Colo.: Johnson Books.

Garment, Leonard

    1997   *Crazy Rhythm: My Journey from Brooklyn, Jazz, and Wall Street to Nixon's White House, Watergate, and Beyond*. New York: Random House.

Garner, Suzanne

    1993   "The Indian Child Welfare Act: A Review." *Wicazo Sa Review* 9 (1):47–51.

Garroutte, Eva Marie

    2003   *Real Indians: Identity and the Survival of Native America*. Berkeley: University of California Press.

Getches, David H., Charles F. Wilkinson, and Robert A. Williams Jr.

    1998   *Cases and Materials on Federal Indian Law*. St. Paul, Minn.: West.

Gillon, Steven M.

    1992   *The Democrats' Dilemma: Walter F. Mondale and the Liberal Legacy*. New York: Columbia University Press.

Goldin, Nicolas S.

    1999   "Casting a New Light on Tribal Casino Gaming: Why Congress Should Curtail the Scope of High Stakes Indian Gaming." *Cornell Law Review* 3:798–854.

González, Ray, ed.

    1992   *Without Discovery: A Native Response to Columbus*. Seattle: Broken Moon Press.

Goodman, Robert
   1995   *The Luck Business: The Devastating Consequences and Broken Prom-*
          ises of America's Gambling Explosion. New York: Free Press.
Gordon-McCutchan, R. C.
   1995   *The Taos Indians and the Battle for Blue Lake.* Santa Fe, N.Mex.: Red
          Crane Books.
Graham, Hugh Davis
   1998   "Civil Rights Policy in the Carter Presidency." In *The Carter Presidency:*
          Policy Choices in the Post–New Deal Era, ed. Gary M. Fink and Hugh
          Davis Graham, 217–18. Lawrence: University Press of Kansas.
Greene, John Robert
   2000   *The Presidency of George Bush.* Lawrence: University Press of Kan-
          sas.
Gross, Emma
   1989   *Contemporary Federal Policy Toward American Indians.* New York:
          Greenwood.
Grounds, Richard A., George E. Tinker, and David E. Wilkins
   2003   *Native Voices: American Indian Identity and Resistance.* Lawrence:
          University Press of Kansas.
Hagan, William T.
   1997   *Theodore Roosevelt and Six Friends of the Indian.* Norman: University
          of Oklahoma Press.
Hanke, Steven H., and Barney Dowdle
   1987   "Privatizing the Public Domain." *Proceedings of the Academy of Po-*
          litical Science 36 (3):114–23.
Hanson, Randel D
   2001   "Half Lives of Reagan's Indian Policy: Marketing Nuclear Waste to
          American Indians." *American Indian Culture and Research Journal*
          25 (1):21–44.
Harjo, Suzan Shown
   1991   "I Won't Be Celebrating Columbus Day." *Newsweek: Columbus*
          Special Issue, Fall/Winter, 32.
Haynal, Patrick
   2000   "Termination and Tribal Survival: The Klamath Tribes of Or-
          egon." *Oregon Historical Quarterly* 101 (3):27–301.
Heclo, Hugh
   1986   "The Political Foundations of Antipoverty Policy." In *Fighting*
          Poverty: What Works and What Doesn't, ed. Sheldon H. Danziger
          and Daniel H. Weinberg, 312–40. Cambridge, Mass.: Harvard Uni-
          versity Press.
Hertzberg, Hazel W.
   1982   "Reaganomics on the Reservation." *New Republic* 187 (November
          22):15–17.
   1988   "Indian Rights Movement, 1887–1973." In *History of Indian-White*

Relations, vol. 4 of *Handbook of North American Indians,* ed. Wilcomb E. Washburn, 305–23. Washington, D.C.: Smithsonian Institution.

Hoxie, Frederick E.

1984   *A Final Promise: The Campaign to Assimilate the Indians, 1890–1920.* Lincoln: University of Nebraska Press.

"Indian Casino Take Is Nearly Twice Nevada's."

2005   *Arizona Daily Star,* February 16, A5.

Iverson, Peter, with Monty Roessel

2002   *Diné: A History of the Navajos.* Albuquerque: University of New Mexico Press.

Johnson, Allen W., and Timothy K. Earle

2000   *The Evolution of Human Societies: From Foraging Group to Agrarian State.* Stanford: Stanford University Press.

Johnson, Tadd M., and James Hamilton

1995   "Self Governance for Indian Tribes: From Paternalism to Empowerment." *Connecticut Law Review* 27 (4):1251–80.

Johnson, Troy R.

1996.   *The Occupation of Alcatraz Island: Indian Self-Determination and the Rise of Indian Activism.* Urbana: University of Illinois Press.

Johnson, Troy R., Joanne Nagel, and Duane Champagne, eds.

1997   *American Indian Activism: Alcatraz to the Longest Walk.* Urbana: University of Illinois Press.

Jones, Charles O.

1988   *The Trusteeship Presidency: Jimmy Carter and the United States Congress.* Baton Rouge: Louisiana State University Press.

Jorgensen, Joseph G.

1986   "Federal Policies, American Indian Polities, and the 'New Federalism.'" *American Indian Culture and Research Journal* 10 (2):1–13.

1998   "Gaming and Recent American Indian Economic Development." *American Indian Culture and Research Journal* 22 (3):157–72.

Josephy, Alvin M., Jr.

1988   "Modern America and the Indian." In *Indians in American History: An Introduction,* ed. Frederick E. Hoxie, 260–71. Arlington Heights, Ill.: Harlan Davidson.

Kammer, Jerry

1980   *The Second Long Walk: The Navajo-Hopi Land Dispute.* Albuquerque: University of New Mexico Press.

Kapur, Carl Costanzo

2004   "Native Hawaiians." In *A Companion to the Anthropology of American Indians,* ed. Thomas Biolsi, 412–32. Oxford: Blackwell Publishing.

Kaufman, Burton I.

1993   *The Presidency of James Earl Carter, Jr.* Lawrence: University Press of Kansas.

Kelly, Lawrence C.
 1975   "The Indian Reorganization Act: The Dream and the Reality." *Pacific Historical Review* 44 (3):291–312.
 1983   *The Assault on Assimilation: John Collier and the Origins of Indian Policy Reform.* Albuquerque: University of New Mexico Press.
Kersey, Harry A., Jr.
 1996   *An Assumption of Sovereignty: Social and Political Transformation among the Florida Seminoles, 1953–1979.* Lincoln: University of Nebraska Press.
Kolb, Charles
 1994   *White House Daze: The Unmaking of Domestic Policy in the Bush Years.* New York: Free Press.
Kvasnicka, Robert M., and Herman J. Viola, eds.
 1979   *The Commissioners of Indian Affairs, 1824–1977.* Lincoln: University of Nebraska Press.
Laffin, Martin
 1996   "The President and the Subcontractors: The Role of Top Level Policy Entrepreneurs in the Bush Administration." *Presidential Studies Quarterly* 26 (2):550–66.
Lammers, William W., and Michael A. Genovese
 2000   *The Presidency and Domestic Policy: Comparing Leadership Styles, FDR to Clinton.* Washington, D.C.: CQ Press.
Lane, Ambrose
 1995   *Return of the Buffalo: The Story Behind America's Indian Gaming Explosion.* Westport, Conn.: Bergin and Garvey.
Lazarus, Edward
 1991   *Black Hills, White Justice.* New York: Harper Collins.
Leuchtenburg, William E.
 1998   "Jimmy Carter and the Post–New Deal Presidency." In *The Carter Presidency: Policy Choices in the Post–New Deal Era,* ed. Gary M. Fink and Hugh Davis Graham, 7–28. Lawrence: University Press of Kansas.
Levin, Stephanie A.
 1997   "Betting on the Land: Indian Gambling and Sovereignty." *Stanford Law and Policy Review* 8 (1):125–39.
Lurie, Nancy Oestrich
 1968   "An American Indian Renascence?" in *The American Indian Today,* ed. Stuart Levine and Nancy Oestrich Lurie, 187–208. Deland, Fla.: Everett Edwards.
MacDonald, Peter, with Ted Schwarz
 1993   *The Last Warrior: Peter MacDonald and the Navajo Nation.* New York: Orion Books.
Manning, Jason
 2001   "Unleashing the Spirit: The Reagan Administration's Indian Policy."

The Ronald Reagan Resource. http://eightiesclub.tripod.com/id394. htm (accessed September 12, 2005).

Mason, W. Dale

2000   *Indian Gaming: Tribal Sovereignty and American Politics.* Norman: University of Oklahoma Press.

Matusow, Allen J.

1984   *The Unraveling of America: A History of Liberalism in the 60s.* New York: Harper.

McClellan, E. Fletcher

1990   "Implementation and Policy Reformulation in Indian Affairs: The Indian Self-Determination and Education Assistance Act of 1975." *Wicazo Sa Review* 6 (1):45–55.

McCool, Daniel

1994   *Command of the Waters: Iron Triangles, Federal Water Development, and Indian Water.* Tucson: University of Arizona Press.

2002   *Native Waters: Contemporary Indian Water Settlements and the Second Treaty Era.* Tucson: University of Arizona Press.

McCulloch, Anne Merline

1994   "The Politics of Indian Gaming: Tribe/State Relations and American Federalism." *Publius* 24 (3):99–122.

McGuire, Thomas R.

1992   "Getting to Yes in the New West." In *State and Reservation: New Perspectives on Federal Indian Policy,* ed. George Castile and Robert Bee, 224–46. Tucson: University of Arizona Press.

McNickle, D'Arcy

1973   *Native American Tribalism: Indian Survival and Renewals.* Oxford; New York: Oxford University Press.

Means, Russell, with Marvin J. Wolf

1995   *Where White Men Fear to Tread: The Autobiography of Russell Means.* New York: St. Martin's Press.

Meighan, Clement W.

1994   "Burying American Archaeology." *Archaeology* 47 (6):64–68.

Merriam, Lewis, ed

1928   *The Problem of Indian Administration.* Baltimore: John Hopkins University Press.

Mervin, David

1996   *George Bush and the Guardianship Presidency.* New York: St. Martin's Press.

Metcalf, Warren R.

2002   *Termination's Legacy: The Discarded Indians of Utah.* Lincoln: University of Nebraska Press.

Miller, Mark Edwin

2004   *Forgotten Tribes: Unrecognized Indians and the Federal Acknowledgment Process.* Lincoln: University of Nebraska Press.

Morris, C. Patrick

    1988   "Termination by Accountants: The Reagan Indian Policy." *Policy Studies Journal* 16 (4):731–50.

Morris, Glenn T.

    2003   "Vine Deloria, Jr., and the Development of a Decolonizing Critique of Indigenous Peoples and International Relations." In *Native Voices: American Indian Identity and Resistance,* ed. Richard A. Grounds, George E. Tinker and David E. Wilkins, 97–154. Lawrence: University Press of Kansas.

Nafziger, James A. R., and Rebecca J. Dobkins

    1999   "The Native American Graves Protection and Repatriation Act in Its First Decade." *International Journal of Cultural Property* 8 (1):77–107.

Nagel, Joane

    1997   *American Indian Ethnic Renewal: Red Power and the Resurgence of Identity and Culture.* New York: Oxford University Press.

NARF [Native American Rights Fund]

    2000   "Federal Recognition of Indian Tribes." *Justice Newsletter* (Fall):2–6.

    2005   "NARF observes 35 years of 'Fighting for Justice.'" *NARF Legal Review* 30 (1):1–6.

Nesper, Larry

    2004   "Treaty Rights." In *A Companion to the Anthropology of American Indians,* ed. Thomas Biolsi, 304–20. Oxford: Blackwell Publishing.

Nichols, Roger L.

    2003   *American Indians in U.S. History.* Norman: University of Oklahoma Press.

Novack, Steven J.

    1990   "The Real Takeover of the BIA: The Preferential Hiring of Indians." *Journal of Economic History* 50 (3):639–54.

Officer, James

    1984   "The Indian Service and Its Evolution." In *The Aggressions of Civilization: Federal Indian Policy since the 1880s,* ed. Vine Deloria Jr. and Sandra Cadwalader, 59–101. Philadelphia: Temple University Press.

Olson, Mary B., and Ada E. Deer

    1982   "Through the 'Safety Net': The Reagan Budget Cuts and the American Indian with a focus on the Menominee Tribe." Paper presented at the Annual Meeting of the Rural Sociological Society, San Francisco.

Parker, Dorothy R.

    1996   *Phoenix Indian School: The Second Half Century.* Tucson: University of Arizona Press.

Parmet, Herbert S.

2000   *George Bush: The Life of a Lone Star Yankee.* New Brunswick, N.J.: Transaction Publishers.

Parsley, John Keith

1993   "Regulation of Counterfeit Indian Arts and Crafts: An Analysis of the Indian Arts and Crafts Act of 1990." *American Indian Law Review* 18 (2):487–514.

Pasquaretta, Paul Andrew

2003   *Gambling and Survival in Native North America.* Tucson: University of Arizona Press.

Passel, Jeffrey S., and Patricia A. Berman

1986   "Quality of 1980 Census Data for Native Americans." *Social Biology* 33 (3–4):163–82.

Patterson, James T.

1994   *America's Struggle Against Poverty, 1900–1994.* Cambridge, Mass.: Harvard University Press.

Pemberton, William E.

1997   *Exit with Honor: The Life and Presidency of Ronald Reagan.* Armonk, N.Y.: M.E. Sharpe.

Peroff, Nicholas

1982   *Menominee Drums: Tribal Termination and Restoration, 1954–1974.* Norman: Oklahoma University Press.

"Peter MacDonald Free after Seven Years."

2001   *Indian Country Today,* January 31.

Pevar, Stephen L.

2002   *The Rights of Indians and Tribes: The Authoritative ACLU Guide to Indian and Tribal Rights.* Carbondale: Southern Illinois University Press.

Philp, Kenneth R.

1977   *John Collier's Crusade for Indian Reform, 1920–1954.* Tucson: University of Arizona Press.

1986   *Indian Self-Rule: First Hand Accounts of Indian-White Relations from Roosevelt to Reagan.* Salt Lake City, Utah: Howe Brothers.

1999   *Termination Revisited: American Indians on the Trail to Self-Determination, 1933–1953.* Lincoln: University of Nebraska Press.

Pickering, Kathleen Ann

2000   *Lakota Culture, World Economy.* Lincoln: University of Nebraska Press.

2004   "Culture and Reservation Economics." In *A Companion to the Anthropology of American Indians,* ed. Thomas Biolsi, 112–29. Oxford: Blackwell Publishers.

Pottinger, Richard

1991   "The American Indian Development Bank?" *American Indian Culture and Research Journal* 16 (1):137–63.

Prucha, Francis Paul

1962   *American Indian Policy in the Formative Years.* Lincoln: University of Nebraska Press.

1976   *American Indian Policy in Crisis: Christian Reformers and the American Indian, 1865–1900.* Norman: University of Oklahoma Press.

1984   *The Great Father: The United States Government and the American Indians.* 2 vols. Lincoln: University of Nebraska Press.

1994   *American Indian Treaties: The History of a Political Anomaly.* Berkeley: University of California Press.

2000   *Documents of United States Indian Policy.* Lincoln: University of Nebraska Press.

Quinn, William W., Jr.

1990   "Federal Acknowledgment of American Indian Tribes: The Historical Development of a Legal Concept." *American Journal of Legal History* 34 (4):331–64.

Quirk, Paul J.

1991   "Domestic Policy: Divided Government and Cooperative Presidential Leadership." In *The Bush Presidency: First Appraisals,* ed. Colin Campbell and Bert A. Rockman, 69–92. Chatham, N.J.: Chatham House.

Rayack, Elton

1987   *Not so Free to Choose: The Political Economy of Milton Friedman and Ronald Reagan.* New York: Praeger.

Reagan, Nancy, with William Novack

1989   *My Turn: The Memoirs of Nancy Reagan.* New York: Random House.

Reagan, Ronald

1980   "Presidential Candidate Reagan Said, September 30, 1980." *Wassaja: The Indian Historian* 13 (3):7.

1990   *Ronald Reagan: An American Life.* New York: Simon and Schuster.

Reid, Harry

1990   "Indian Gaming and the Law." In *Indian Gaming and the Law,* ed. William R. Eadington, 15–20. Reno: Institute for the Study of Gambling and Commercial Gaming, College of Business Administration, University of Nevada.

Reyner, Jon, and Jeanne Eder

2004   *American Indian Education: A History.* Norman: University of Oklahoma Press.

Roberts, Randy, and James S. Olson

1995   *John Wayne: American.* New York: Free Press.

Rose, I. Nelson

1990   "Indian Gaming and the Law" In *Indian Gaming and the Law,* ed. William R. Eadington, 3–14. Reno: Institute for the Study of Gambling and Commercial Gaming, College of Business Administration, University of Nevada.

Rosenbaum, Herbert D., and Alexej Ugrinsky, eds
1997   *The Presidency and Domestic Policies of Jimmy Carter.* Westport, Conn.: Greenwood Press.

Schrader, Robert Fay
1983   *The Indian Arts and Crafts Board: An Aspect of Indian New Deal Policy.* Albuquerque: University of New Mexico Press.

Schulte, Steven C.
1984   "Removing the Yoke of Government: E. Y. Berry and the Origins of Indian Termination Policy." *South Dakota History* 14 (1):48–67.

Service, Elman
1962   *Primitive Social Organization: An Evolutionary Perspective.* New York: Random House.

Sharamitaro, Lisa M.
2001   "Association Involvement across the Policy Process: The American Association of Museums and the Native American Graves Protection and Repatriation Act." *The Journal of Arts Management, Law and Society* 31 (2):123–36.

Sheffield, Gail
1997   *The Arbitrary Indian: The Indian Arts and Crafts Act of 1990.* Norman: University of Oklahoma Press.

Sheffield, R. Scott
2004   *The Red Man's on the Warpath: The Image of the "Indian" and the Second World War.* Vancouver: UBC press.

Short, C. Brant
1989   *Ronald Reagan and the Public Lands: America's Conservation Debate, 1979–1984.* College Station: Texas A&M University Press.

Shull, Steven A.
1993   *A Kinder Gentler Racism? The Reagan-Bush Civil Rights Legacy.* Armonk, N.Y.: M.E. Sharpe.

Sider, Gerald M.
1993   *Lumbee Indian Histories: Race, Ethnicity, and Indian Identity in the Southern United States.* New York: Cambridge University Press.

Slotkin, Richard
1992   *Gunfighter Nation: The Myth of the Frontier in Twentieth Century America.* New York: Athenaeum.

Smith, Paul Chaat, and Robert Allen Warrior
1996   *Like a Hurricane: The Indian Movement from Alcatraz to Wounded Knee.* New York: The New Press.

Spicer, Edward H.
1940   *Pascua: A Yaqui Village in Arizona.* Chicago: University of Chicago Press.

1969   *A Short History of the Indians of the United States.* New York: Van Nostrand.

1980   *The Yaquis: A Cultural History.* Tucson: University of Arizona Press.

Spilde, Katherine A.

1999   "Indian Gaming Study." *Anthropology Newsletter* 40 (4):11–16.

Stearn, John

2005   "Navajos Seek Gaming Director: Tribe Prepares to Launch 1st Casino." *Arizona Republic,* March 4, D1.

Stripes, James

1999   "A Strategy of Resistance: The 'Actorvism' of Russell Means from Plymouth Rock to Disney Studios." *Wicazo Sa Review.* 14 (1):87–101.

Strober, Deborah Hart, and Gerald S. Strober

1998   *Reagan: The Man and His Presidency.* Boston: Houghton Mifflin.

Stuart, Paul H.

1990   "Financing Self-Determination: Federal Indian Expenditures, 1975–1988." *American Indian Culture and Research Journal* 14 (2):1–18.

Stull, Donald D.

1990   "Reservation Economic Development in the Era of Self-Determination." *American Anthropologist* 92 (1):206–10.

Stull, Donald D., Jerry A. Schultz, and Ken Cadue Sr.

1986   "Rights without Resources: The Rise and Fall of the Kansas Kickapoo." *American Indian Culture and Research Journal* 10 (2):41–59.

Sugrue, Thomas J.

1998   "Carter's Urban Policy Crisis." In *The Carter Presidency: Policy Choices in the Post–New Deal Era,* ed. Gary M. Fink and Hugh Davis Graham, 137–57. Lawrence: University Press of Kansas.

Sutton, Imre

2001   "Tribes and States: A Political Geography of Indian Environmental Jurisdiction." In *Trusteeship in Change: Toward Tribal Autonomy in Resource Management,* ed. Richmond L. Clow and Imre Sutton, 239–63. Boulder: University of Colorado Press.

Swimmer, Ross O.

1989   "A Blueprint for Economic Development in Indian Country." *Journal of Energy Law and Policy* 10 (1):13–31.

Szasz, Margaret Connell

1999   *Education and the American Indian: The Road to Self-Determination since 1928.* Albuquerque: University of New Mexico Press.

Taylor, Graham

1980   *The New Deal and American Indian Tribalism: The Administration of the Indian Reorganization Act, 1934–45.* Lincoln: University of Nebraska Press.

Taylor, Theodore W.

1983   *American Indian Policy.* Mt. Airy, Md.: Lomond Publications.

Thomas, David Hurst

2000   *Skull Wars: Kennewick Man, Archaeology, and the Battle for Native American Identity.* New York: Basic Books.

Thompson, Mark

1979   "Nurturing the Forked Tree: Conception and Formation of the American Indian Policy Review Commission." In *New Directions in Federal Indian Policy: A Review of the American Indian Policy Review Commission.* American Indian Study Center. Los Angeles: University of California Press.

Tiefer, Charles

1994   *The Semi-Sovereign Presidency: The Bush Administration's Strategy for Governing without Congress.* Boulder, Colo.: Westview.

Time

1993   "Jail Time." *Time*, March 1, p. 11.

Townsend, Kenneth William

2000   *World War II and the American Indian.* Albuquerque: University of New Mexico Press.

Trahant, M. N., A. Hall, and M. Schaffer

1987   "Fraud in Indian Country: A Billion Dollar Betrayal." *Arizona Republic,* October 4–11.

Trennert, Robert A.

1988   *The Phoenix Indian School: Forced Assimilation in Arizona, 1891–1935.* Norman: University of Oklahoma Press.

Trope, Jack F. and Walter R. Echo-Hawk

2001   "The Native American Graves Protection and Repatriation Act: Background and Legislative History." In *The Future of the Past: Archaeologists, Native Americans, and Repatriation,* ed. Tamara L. Bray, 9–34. New York: Garland.

Vaughn, Stephen

1994   *Ronald Reagan in Hollywood: Movies and Politics.* Cambridge; New York: Cambridge University Press.

Viola, Herman J.

2002   *Ben Nighthorse Campbell: An American Warrior.* Boulder, Colo.: Johnson Books.

Vizenor, Gerald

1992   "Gambling on Sovereignty." *American Indian Quarterly* 16 (3):411–13.

Wallace, Anthony

1993   *The Long Bitter Trail.* New York: Hill and Wang.

Warshaw, Shirley Anne

1997   "The Carter Experience with Cabinet Government." In *The Presidency and Domestic Policies of Jimmy Carter,* ed. Herbert D. Rosenbaum and Alexej Uginsky. Westport, Conn.: Greenwood Press.

Washburn, Wilcomb E.

1975   *The Assault on Indian Tribalism: The General Allotment Law (Dawes Act) of 1887*. Philadelphia: Lippincott.

Watson, Ben

1995   *Frank Zappa: The Negative Dialectics of Poodle Play*. New York: St. Martin's Press.

Watt, James G., with Doug Wead

1985   *The Courage of a Conservative*. New York: Simon and Schuster.

Weisbrot, Robert

1990   *Freedom Bound: A History of the American Civil Rights Movement*. New York: Norton.

Wesley, Clarence

1954   "Tribal Self Government Under the IRA." In *Indian Affairs and the Indian Reorganization Act: The Twenty Year Record*, ed. William H. Kell, 26–28. Tucson: University of Arizona Press.

White, Richard

1991   *"It's Your Misfortune and None of My Own": A New History of the American West*. Norman: University of Oklahoma Press.

Wilkins, David E.

1995   "The 'De-Selected' Senate Committee on Indian Affairs and its Legislative Record, 1977–1992." *European Review of Native American Studies* 9 (1):27–34.

2002   *American Indian Politics and the American Political System*. Lanham, Md.: Rowman and Littlefield.

2003   *The Navajo Political Experience*. Lanham, Md.: Rowman and Littlefield.

Wilkins, David E., and K. Tsianina Lomawaima

2001   *Uneven Ground: American Indian Sovereignty and Federal Law*. Norman: University of Oklahoma Press.

Wilkinson, Charles

2005   *Blood Struggle: The Rise of Modern Indian Nations*. New York: Norton and Co.

Williams, Robert A., Jr.

1990   *The American Indian in Western Legal Thought: The Discourses of Conquest*. Oxford: Oxford University Press.

Williamson, Richard S.

1990   *Reagan's Federalism: His Efforts to Decentralize Government*. Lanham, Md.: University Press of America.

Index

Abourezk, James, 27, 29, 32–33, 36, 37, 38, 46, 48, 124n2; and American Indian Policy Review Commission, 34–35; and Federal Acknowledgment Process, 40, 41; and Pascua Yaquis, 44–45
activism: American Indian Movement, 47, 48, 92–93; political, 11, 12–13
adoption, 36–37
affirmative action, 59
AIM. *See* American Indian Movement
AIPRC. *See* American Indian Policy Review Commission
AIRFA. *See* American Indian Religious Freedom Act
Ak-Chin bill, 25
Ak-Chin settlement, 67–68
Alaska, 38, 70
Alaska National Interest Lands Conservation Act (ANILCA), 30, 124n37
Alaska Native Claims Settlement Act, 90, 104
Alaska Native Commission, 104
Alcatraz Island: sit-in on, 13, 47
Alderman, Cliff, 96
American Association of Museums, 106
American Indian Day, 56
American Indian Movement (AIM), 47, 48, 92–93
American Indian Policy Review

Commission (AIPRC), 30, 33, 40; role of, 34–36
American Indian Religious Freedom Act (AIRFA), 30, 89–90
American Indian Religious Freedom resolution, 37
American Museum of Natural History, 104
Ancient Indian Land Claims Settlement Act, 66
Andrade, Ron, 54, 55
Andrews, Mark, 73
Andrus, Cecil, 18, 20, 21, 45
ANILCA, 30, 124n37
Antiquities Act, 38
Apaches: federal administration of, 5–6
Archaeological Resources Protection Act, 30, 38, 106
arts and crafts: regulating authenticity of, 106–7
assimilation: forced, 6
Association on American Indian Affairs, 36
austerity measures: of President Carter, 27–28

Banks, Dennis, 48
BAR, 42
Barron-Collier Company, 70
Benedict, Jeff, 68–69
Berg, David, 17
Berry, E. Y., 10

About the Author

George Pierre Castile is professor of anthropology at Whitman College. His publications include *To Show Heart: Native American Self-Determination and Federal Indian Policy, 1960–1975* and *State and Reservation: New Perspectives on Federal Indian Policy* (co-editor with Robert L. Bee), both published by the University of Arizona Press.